Roots of the
Western Tradition

ROOTS OF THE WESTERN TRADITION:

A Short History of the Ancient World
Fourth Edition

C. WARREN HOLLISTER

University of California, Santa Barbara

JOHN WILEY & SONS

New York   Chichester   Brisbane   Toronto   Singapore

Library of Congress Cataloging in Publication Data:

Hollister, C. Warren (Charles Warren), 1930–
  Roots of the Warren tradition.

  Includes bibliographical references and index.
  1. History, Ancient. I. Title.
D59.H64   1982   930   81-23141
ISBN 0-471-08900-1 (pbk.) AACR2

Printed in the United States of America

10 9 8 7 6 5 4 3 2 1

About the Author

C. Warren Hollister, Professor of History at the University of California, Santa Barbara, received his BA from Harvard and his MA and Ph.D. from UCLA. He is a Fellow of the Medieval Academy of America and the Royal Historical Society (London) and has served as Vice-President for Teaching of the American Historical Association, President of the Pacific Coast Conference on British Studies, Visiting Research Fellow of Merton College, Oxford, and Visiting Fellow of the Australian National University. The author of many scholarly books and articles, and co-author of a children's fantasy, he has been honored with Guggenheim, NEH, Fulbright, ACLS, and American Philosophical Society Fellowships. He has lectured at numerous colleges and universities across America and at such overseas universities as Cambridge, Oxford, Ghent, Leyden, Utrecht, London, Sydney, Auckland, Tasmania, Bologna, and Moscow. He is currently on the editorial boards of the *American Historical Review, Albion,* the *Journal of Medieval History,* and the University of California Press. He serves on the National Advisory Board of the Society for History Education and chairs the National Development Committee for the College Board Advanced Placement Test in European History. Among his other honors are the Triennial Book Prize of the Conference on British Studies, the E. Harris Harbison National Award for Distinguished Teaching, and the Walter D. Love Memorial Prize of 1981 for the best scholarly article in any area of British history or culture.

Preface

This fourth edition of *Roots of the Western Tradition* has undergone a page-by-page, word-by-word revision to achieve greater clarity and accuracy and to incorporate the results of recent research. The Introduction and Chapter 1 are rewritten completely, and Chapters 2, 4, 11, and 15 are heavily revised. Ancient history is more vulnerable to scholarly revision than most other historical fields because of the relative scarcity of documents and the growing momentum of archeological investigations. Entire civilizations have turned up since I prepared the third edition of *Roots*, and it is unsettling to realize that one or two new ones could be unearthed between the writing of this present edition and its publication. As a result of constant discoveries and reinterpretations by historians and archeologists throughout the world, not a page of this edition remains unchanged from the last.

Specifically, I have incorporated major revisions into my treatments of the Paleolithic and Neolithic eras, the emergence of cities and civilizations, Mesopotamia and its urban neighbors to the east (Iran) and west (Ebla), the Hittites and other Indo-Europeans, the Minoans, the Mycenaean and Dorian Greeks, Greek religion, the Greek economy and society, the reforms of Cleisthenes, the battle of Salamis, the Macedonians, Ptolemaic Egypt, Hellenistic society and culture, class relationships in republican Rome, the culture of the Roman silver age, the rise of Christianity, and the barbarian invasions. On the disintegration of Roman authority in the West, I have adopted the current gradualist approach but have drawn back from the recent suggestion that "what we call the Fall of the Western Empire was an imaginative experiment that got a little out of hand." The place of women in ancient societies has received added emphasis throughout.

In this edition, as in previous ones, it has been my goal to strike a proper balance between factual narrative and interpretation, to maintain the highest possible level of accuracy, to present sound, current interpretations, and to write clearly and, if possible, vividly. Above all, I have tried to be brief, believing that beginning college students need a genial and agile guide through ancient history rather than an encyclopedic catalogue of facts. With the conviction that the great textbook has yet to be written, I have tried at least to write a succinct one that will leave adequate time for the student to pursue extensive collateral reading. Annotated guides to such reading, both in modern works and in the original sources, are provided at the ends of the three parts into which this book is divided.

I am particularly fortunate in having as my friends and colleagues at Santa Barbara such distinguished specialists as Brian M. Fagan (prehistoric and ancient archeology), Frank J. Frost (ancient Greece), and Harold Drake (ancient Rome), all of whom helped keep me current with the most recent scholarship by answering my frequent inquiries with authority and good cheer. Frank Frost put the third edition of *Roots* under his critical microscope, and his detailed comments were immensely helpful to me in preparing this present book. I am also much indebted to other scholars for their thorough and valuable comments on earlier editions: Harold Drake (again), Mortimer Chambers, Judy Turner, and William G. Sinnigen. All remaining blunders are mine, not theirs. I also thank my research assistants, past and present: Alberto Ferreiro, Professor Sally N. Vaughn, and Professor Thomas K. Keefe.

C. Warren Hollister
University of California,
Santa Barbara

Contents

List of Maps

Maps by Russell H. Lenz

List of Illustrations

Introduction: The Western Tradition

Some people are rather like ants. They work together at tasks that ensure the survival and prosperity of the anthill, never wondering why. Ants have several good excuses. They are governed primarily by instinct, not by an evolving culture that must be absorbed over a period of years. Were some super-ant to develop an interest in anthill history, or in the study of comparative anthills, the result would be most discouraging. Individual anthills come and go, but anthill society does not change through time. One anthill has been much like another since the days of the first ants.

Human beings, on the other hand, are products of sweeping cultural changes that stretch back countless thousands of years. In our own time, the pace has become so swift that some people see no point in studying history at all. Because the past is altogether different from the present, they argue, nothing that happened before 1960 (or 1945, 1914, or whenever) can possibly be relevant now. On this same flabby reasoning, one needn't bother with such impractical things as Shakespearian drama, nineteenth-century novels, archeology, or astronomy. Who cares where we are in time or space, or where we come from? The anthill beckons.

But with the exception of some first-generation immigrants, every American is the product of a Western cultural tradition so encompassing that we scarcely notice it—as a fish is unaware of the ocean in which it swims. Our culture shapes our assumptions, defines our options, and governs the very categories in which we judge and perceive. And there is no escaping it. A Communist revolutionary is expressing the Western tradition of social protest in terms of the doctrine of Karl Marx, a Western intellectual of the last century. An anthropologist investigating preliterate non-Western cultures is engaging in a typically Western enterprise; non-Western cultures have not produced anthropologists except under Western stimulus. Indeed, the overwhelming majority of courses and majors offered by a modern university consist of various strands in the Western cultural fabric. The natural sciences, social sciences, arts, and humanities are all deeply rooted in Western Europe—and in non-European lands such as our own that have felt its influence. The university is itself a Western invention.

This is certainly not to suggest that Western culture is superior to others, but simply to recognize that American society in the 1980s remains firmly under its spell. The study of non-Western cultures, valuable and liberating in itself, has the further advantage of placing the Western tradition in a much broader perspective. Our understanding of our own culture is enriched by viewing it in the context of other cultures, just as our understanding of ourselves as individuals depends on our knowledge of other people. But we must begin at home. Without some sense of what it means to be "Western," the term "non-Western" is, quite obviously, drained of its meaning.

The Western cultural tradition stretches back some 1200 years or more into the European past. It rose from the debris of a still older civilization—the Greco-Roman—from which it derived much of its political, artistic, and philosophical tone. Western Civilization drew also from the Judeo-Christian tradition of the ancient Near East, which was inspired in part by the still earlier religious thought of Mesopotamia, Egypt, and the lands between. Greco-Roman Civilization was itself a child of former cultures: Minoan, Etruscan, and, behind them, Egyptian and Mesopotamian. This connected sequence of civilizations extends, like an immense chain, backward some six thousand years to Mesopotamia's emergence from the Stone Age and forward into an unmapped future.

This book will deal with Western Europe's cultural antecedents—the civilizations of the ancient Near East, Greece, and Rome. These early cultures contributed decisively to the rise of the West. Without them we would not exist. They are the deep roots from which our civilization has grown.

PART
1

THE ANCIENT
NEAR EAST

Chapter
1

The Stone Age and the Birth of Civilizations

THE OLD STONE AGE

Relative to the total time span of the human race, civilization is a latecomer. In 1981 a team of archeologists reported the discovery, in an Ethiopian gully, of primitive stone tools dating back at least two and a half million years—half a million years earlier than any previous finds. The tools are very crude: 48 small, sharp-edged slivers of volcanic stone and three fist-sized cutters, probably designed to hack through the skins of animals and to butcher their carcasses. The concentration of these tools at a single site suggests a home base for a band of prowling hunters.

Humans alone of all creatures are capable of making tools and using them purposefully. Anthropologists describe the earliest toolmakers (collectively) as *Homo habilis,* "the skillful man." The tool-making breakthrough of *Homo habilis* was made possible by a relatively large brain and agile hands, cunningly contrived for the grasping of objects. But the earliest humans differed markedly from people of today in height, brain size, and general physical makeup. Gradually, across thousands and millions of years, brains grew and tools improved. People learned how to make fire and control it; they manufactured stone axes; they invented coherent speech; they sought to tame the savage, perverse forces of nature by developing religions. *Homo habilis* developed slowly, through uneven stages, into *Homo sapiens,* "the man who knows"—the prototype of all people of all races living today.

Long after the emergence of *Homo sapiens* some 75,000 years ago, the human economy continued to be based, as always before, on hunting, fishing, and gathering wild foods. For well over ninety-nine percent of its existence on earth, humanity lived in what has been called the Paleolithic, or Old Stone Age. Progress was far too slow to be recognized as such, and life was desperately insecure. But progress there was. Toward the end of the Paleolithic era (about 30,000 to 10,000 years ago) a *Homo sapiens* race living on the continent of Europe, known as Cro-Magnon man, carried the art of hunting to new levels of efficiency. A Cro-Magnon site in Czechoslovakia contains the skeletons of a thousand hairy mammoths, and a site in France testifies to the killing of tens of thousands of horses.

One of the dazzling achievements of Cro-Magnon culture was its cave paintings. In caverns such as those at Lascaux in France and Altamira in Spain, walls are ablaze with boldly realistic portrayals of animals—the woolly rhinoceros, the reindeer, the hairy mammoth—painted with assurance and skill, and enlivened with bright earth colors. These drawings may well have had some magical intent, perhaps to aid in the hunt by depicting and thereby bewitching the hunted beasts. It would be attractive, though doubtless naive, to imagine Cro-Magnon painters producing art for its own sake. But whatever their purpose, the cave paintings occupy a unique place at the dawn of human art. The mastery of draftsmanship that they display would not be duplicated for thousands of years.

The inhabitants of late-Paleolithic Europe were sculptors as well. They were fond of producing stone statuettes of women, often with exaggerated breasts, buttocks, and genitals. Modern archeologists refer to them as "Venuses." Perhaps they represent a fertility goddess; we can only guess. One late-Paleolithic Venus from southwestern France holds a bison horn, shaped like a crescent moon and marked with thirteen lines. Similar groups of markings found on the tusks of hairy mammoths, on rocks, on ivory staffs, and on the bones of animals and birds, suggest the possibility that late-Paleolithic peoples had developed a lunar calendar (of thirteen months per year) in order to plan their hunting and food gathering by anticipating changes of season. If so, the inhabitants of late-Stone-Age Europe were bringing their activities under a degree of rational control unknown to all previous ages of human existence.

The appearance of the reindeer and hairy mammoth in late-Paleolithic art bears witness to an environment far colder than today's. The Cro-Magnons inhabited Europe during the last of a drawn-out series of glacial ages, during which Arctic glaciers moved slowly southward to cover large portions of Europe, Asia, and North America with deep blankets of ice.

Gradually, between about 10,000 and 8,000 B.C., the last glaciation receded to the Arctic. Europe grew warmer, and the garden lands of North Africa and the Near East underwent a long drying-out period. Reindeer migrated northward out of Europe and America, never to return (or at most, as some suppose, one night a year). The woolly rhinoceros and hairy mammoth became extinct, living on only in the galleries of Altamira and Lascaux. Cro-Magnon culture died out too, as new peoples settled across Europe and the Near East, with new weapons (bows and arrows) and a new maritime technology (canoes, nets, fishing lines.)

By transforming the environment, the advance and retreat of the glaciers prevented human societies from becoming permanently set in their ways. Without the ice ages, Paleolithic culture might well have continued indefinitely.

THE NEOLITHIC REVOLUTION

Around 8000 B.C. the initial steps were taken, in a few localities in the Near East, toward the greatest revolution humanity had yet experienced: the development of agriculture. Very likely the revolution resulted from the ingenuity of women, gathering wild grain while the men were off hunting, and discovering the uses of seed. This momentous advance ushered in what is known as the Neolithic or New Stone Age and has aptly been termed "the Neolithic Revolution."

The emergence of farming, together with the concurrent domestication of animals for food, enabled people for the first time to live in large, settled communities, to build permanent shelters, and to control their food supply. After two and a half million precarious years of hunting and gathering food, people were learning at last to produce it themselves.

The Neolithic Revolution spread gradually through the Near East and then, slowly and unevenly, across much of the world. Wherever it occurred, the advent of agriculture and animal domestication transformed human life by providing a far more dependable and abundant food supply. The dramatic rise in the quantity and quality of food (wheat and barley, sheep, goat cheese) generated a surge in population and set the stage for the emergence, a few thousand years later, of the first civilizations.

The new Neolithic villages required a more complex social organization than had existed before. Their inhabitants had to make rational plans to till their soil, breed and slaughter their animals, defend their homes and food against raiding expeditions, and appease their moody gods. The invention of pottery early in the Neolithic era made it possible to store and transport liquids, and created the need for an expanding new group of specialists—the potters. Indeed, village life gave rise to an increasing specialization of labor to perform a variety of essential tasks. And the coordination of all these tasks required supervision and direction. Gradually political institutions developed, with leadership in the hands of warriors and priests. The warriors possessed the weapons; the priests appeased the gods; and the others, having no such power, obeyed.

By the middle of the fifth millennium before Christ (about 4500 B.C.), Neolithic villages were scattered over the lands of present-day Iran, Iraq, Syria, Palestine, Turkey, and Egypt. The earliest major Neolithic village thus far unearthed, at Jericho in Palestine, has been dated by radiocarbon analysis to about 7800

B.C. Here, on the eight-acre site, some 3,000 inhabitants lived in round houses with cone-shaped roofs, like the homes of the Munchkins in Oz. Neolithic Jericho was dominated by a columned temple in which archeologists have found numerous figurines of baked mud representing animals, a man, a woman, and an infant boy. Pottery has been found only in later levels of the site; in 7800 B.C. the pot had yet to be invented. Some thousand years later, Jericho had become a fortified town surrounded by a moat and a stone wall with a protective tower. By then, some strong central authority was clearly in charge of things.

Pottery abounded in the village at Catal Huyuk in southern Turkey, a twenty-five acre site dated to around 6500 B.C. Here the villagers wove wool into cloth, ate more varied food (peas, nuts, vegetable oil, apples, and honey, besides the usual grain cereals), and boasted a formidable weapons technology (sharper flint spearheads and arrowheads, daggers and lances). During the 1960s several Neolithic villages were discovered in Iran, some of which could be even older than Jericho, though smaller and more primitive. In 1967 a larger site, dating to 4500 B.C., was found at Tepe Yahya in south-central Iran, containing pottery, bone-handled sickles, and a remarkable fertility symbol—a green stone phallus carved in the shape of a woman. At Jarmo in Iraq, a village about as old as Tepe Yahya, archeologists have discovered stone bracelets, beads, and tools in such abundance and variety as to suggest that craft specialization was by then far advanced.

These Neolithic villages disclose successive revolutionary changes in human culture. By modern standards the advance was terribly slow. But judged by the span of human existence across the vast Paleolithic era, the invention of agriculture had sparked a chain reaction: animal domestication, temples, pottery, weaving, craft specialization, fearsome new weapons, and political centralization.

Across the fifth millennium, the culture of the Neolithic villages moved ahead step by step. The site at Jarmo discloses twelve separate levels of settlement, and its later levels attest clearly to a more varied craftsmanship and a higher technology. At Jarmo and elsewhere, materials such as obsidian, which were not available locally, suggest the existence of interregional commerce. And by 4000 B.C. the inhabitants of some Neolithic villages were beginning to use copper tools.

We have now reached the threshold of civilization. The coming millennium—4000–3000 B.C.—would see the building of the world's first cities, the development of large-scale irrigation systems along the Tigris and Euphrates Rivers in Mesopotamia and the Nile in Egypt, the invention of writing, the birth of the state, and the smelting of tin and copper into bronze—a much stronger metal than any known before. Thenceforth, throughout most of the Near East, bronze replaced stone in the making of weapons and tools. The Stone Age drew to an end at last, and the Bronze Age commenced.

THE COMING OF CIVILIZATION

Civilization has been defined in various ways. The word is derived from the Latin *civitas*—city—and it is true that urban life is a vital component of what we know as civilization. In antiquity, city dwellers constituted only a minority of the population of a civilized region, but they dominated its political and cultural life. The city was the focal point of political authority, tax collection, commerce, religious practice, intellectual activity, literature, and art. Townspeople were thus a privileged group that had won release from the age-long burdens of gathering and producing food. Whether rich or poor, they owed their existence to the agricultural abundance of the surrounding countryside, which they siphoned off through taxes, tribute, and the profits of commerce. A cynic might reflect that they had domesticated their farm workers in much the way that earlier peoples had domesticated their animals.

Another characteristic of the earliest civilizations was their use of metal weapons and tools. The birth of civilization is more or less concurrent with the coming of the Bronze Age. As one might guess, bronze was rarer and much more expensive than stone, and its use was limited largely to the military and priestly elites. Among the lower social orders, the Stone Age dragged on.

Writing was still another mark of civilization. At the Mesopotamian city of Uruk in about 3500 B.C., temple scribes were keeping accounts in the first known examples of picture writing. With the coming of written records, humanity acquired the means of keeping track of its affairs, and its past, with tremendously greater precision and reliability than ever before. The dim world of campfire legend began to brighten with the oncoming dawn of recorded history.

During the fourth millennium, writing, bronze metallurgy, and city life emerged concurrently—first in Mesopotamia, then in Iran and Egypt. The process was duplicated around 2500 B.C. in the Indus Valley in India, and again some 800 or 1000 years later on the banks of the Huang Ho (Yellow) River in China. Egypt and Iran may have been influenced by the slightly earlier Mesopotamian example, and Mesopotamia may also have provided certain stimuli to the earliest civilization along the Indus River (though the issue is far from settled). But if Chinese civilization owed anything to external models, the evidence eludes us. And the emergence of civilization in the Americas, much later on, was obviously unaided by Afro-Asian precedents.

Scholars are more inclined to view the birth of most Old World civilizations as a series of more or less independent responses, by widely separated Neolithic peoples, to the challenge of clearing, diking, and irrigating river valleys. The periodic flooding of the rivers—the Tigris-Euphrates, Nile, Indus, and Huang Ho—spread rich silt across their valleys, making them singularly and permanently fertile. But the valleys could not be settled and exploited until the floods were brought under control and the water distributed by large-scale irrigation systems. Neolithic technological advances opened the way, but the taming of the river valleys was by no means inevitable. It demanded a degree of coordinated human effort far beyond the capacity of a Neolithic village society. The task could be accomplished only by a centralized political authority controlling large numbers of people and large stretches of land. The establishment of such authority brought with it the first city states and earliest civilizations.

Chapter
2

Mesopotamia

CIVILIZATION EMERGES IN MESOPOTAMIA: 4000–2350 B.C.

Mesopotamia lies in the valley formed by two neighboring rivers, the Tigris and Euphrates. The name is derived from the Greek *mesos* (middle) and *potamoi* (rivers) and means, literally, "between the rivers." The birth of civilization in this region can best be understood by looking at Mesopotamia's geography, environment, and culture during the fourth millennium.

For thousands of years the entire Near East had experienced steadily decreasing rainfall. Grasslands slowly became desert wastes; the valleys of the Nile and the Tigris-Euphrates, once densely overgrown swamps, gradually became habitable. As the accompanying map shows, the Tigris-Euphrates Valley is actually a long strip of fertile lowlands with a highland region to the

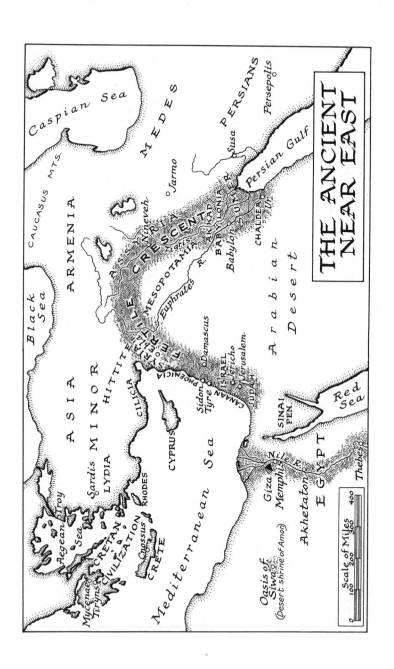

THE ANCIENT NEAR EAST

Scale of Miles
0   100 200 300 400

northeast and the Arabian Desert to the southwest. The rich lowlands of the valley form the eastern part of a large semicircular region whose western extremity runs along the eastern Mediterranean coast. This "Fertile Crescent," arching northward from the Mediterranean and the Persian Gulf, was throughout history an alluring prize for both the northern hill peoples and the southern desert peoples.

Most of the earliest Neolithic villages were established in the high country to the northeast, which had long been attracting settlers because of its fertile soil, adequate rainfall, and native grasses—wheat and barley. The valley itself presented special problems. Its soil, replenished annually by the rich silt of the flooding rivers, was vastly more fertile than the soil of the neighboring hills, but the swamps had to be drained, the water of the rivers had to be distributed over the dry land, and above all the destructive floods had to be mastered.

The valley presented its inhabitants with both a mission and a reward. Drainage systems would control the floods, thereby making settled life bearable, and would also bring water to the thirsty soil. Once these systems were built, the ever-renewed soil would produce crops in such abundance as the hill dwellers had never imagined. The Neolithic villages were simply inadequate to this task, but larger communities emerged that were able to direct sizable quantities of labor toward a common goal and to irrigate large areas. As a consequence of these efforts, the rich land produced a surplus, and the wealth was thereby created with which the new states could expand. No longer was everybody obliged to work the soil; other careers were now possible. The vast majority remained on the land, as they would until recent times, but a crucially important minority began to specialize in such things as war, administration, handicrafts, trade, and service to the gods.

Such was the process that produced civilization. The evolution can be understood in part as a series of historical causes and effects, but at the core of the matter there remains an element of mystery—of volition—perhaps even courage. One can analyze in retrospect the possibilities of the situation, but one cannot explain adequately why they were grasped and exploited by those specific people at that specific time.

THE SUMERIANS

The people who built the earliest civilization in Mesopotamia are known as Sumerians. Their language, probably the first human tongue to be expressed in writing, differed radically from the dialects spoken by the Semitic peoples who were to play a central role in later Mesopotamian history. The culture of the Sumerians outlasted its creators to become the nucleus of all later Mesopotamian civilization. Their architecture, their mode of writing, their literary and artistic styles, and their attitude toward life and toward the gods persevered in the Valley of the Two Rivers and its neighboring lands throughout antiquity.

The outlook of the Sumerians and their successors was deeply pessimistic. Nobody can say exactly why this was so, but the Mesopotamian environment doubtless had something to do with it. To the ancient Mesopotamians, nature seemed violent and unpredictable. No matter how they tried, they could never completely tame the fitful and uneven floods. Sometimes the water level would be inadequate, and drought would result. At other times raging waters might break through the levees and submerge whole towns. As late as A.D. 1831, the rampaging Tigris burst its dikes and swept into Baghdad, annihilating seven thousand homes in one night.

Mesopotamia was a land of extreme contrasts. Weeks of blistering heat might be followed by torrential rains that turned field into marshland and immobilized the population. There were furious winds and suffocating dust storms. Worse still, the fertile valley was open to incessant raids and periodic conquests by envious tribes from the northern hills or the southern desert. In short, the price of civilization in Mesopotamia was constant insecurity.

RELIGION AND CULTURE

The Sumerians projected this ever-present dread into their conceptions of humanity and its gods. Early peoples tended to regard all inanimate objects as personalities with wills of their own. Mountains, trees, rivers, even sticks and stones, were alive and had volition. The more spectacular aspects of nature—the wind, the sky, the earth—were usually regarded as gods. Today people see the world around them as inanimate—as an "it"—but primitive peoples thought of the world as animate—as a "thou." To them, humanity and nature were linked by an "I-thou" relationship.

The Sumerians, awed and terrorized by nature, saw themselves as its plaything. They were impotent before its invincible powers, tragic figures subject to the whims of the gods. "Mere man—," the Sumerians observed, "his days are numbered; whatever he may do, he is but wind." The delights of heaven were not for humans; the scanty allusions to the afterlife in Mesopotamian literature represent it as a state of darkness and gloom.

Being an agricultural people, the Sumerians recognized the regularity of nature, the daily sweep of the sun, and the annual procession of the seasons that governed the rhythm of planting and harvesting. Their chief deity was the sky god, Anu, and their most beloved was the earth goddess, Inanna, who symbolized fertility. The worship of the Earth Mother is a product of the Neolithic Revolution, when the invention of farming suddenly made the fertility of the soil all important; she is perhaps represented by the female statuettes discovered in various Neolithic villages, and she retained her importance (under a variety of names) throughout antiquity. But the Sumerians had other deities less benign than those of earth and sky. Enlil, the god of storms, symbolized destruction, wildness, and violence. Against the orderly sequence of crops and seasons, Enlil represented nature's terrifying, unpredictable side.

Helpless before the wrath of the elements, Sumerians saw themselves as slaves to the gods. This theme of human bondage appears vividly in the Mesopotamian Epic of Creation, where it is said, "Let man be burdened with the gods' toil, that the gods may freely breathe." The Sumerians honored the gods whom they served by building great temples in the centers of their city-states. The temple priests controlled much of the land and labor of the city-states' inhabitants. Indeed, it was in the service of the temples and their gods that the Sumerians made many of their most fundamental contributions to civilization.

The temple buildings themselves constitute humanity's earliest efforts at monumental architecture. Most of them were built on terraced artifical mounds called ziggurats that may have been intended to represent mountains. To the Sumerians, the mountain was the source of the earth's potency and as such constituted an intensely significant religious symbol. The terraced or set-back style of the ziggurat temple and of most other large-scale Mesopotamian architecture was partly dictated by the clay brick that was the chief building material in a land where stone and wood were scarce. The use of clay bricks by Mesopotamian builders gave rise to such basic architectural forms as the arch.

The first Sumerian writing was done by temple scribes who began to keep accounts of the considerable economic resources of their temples. Such were the mundane beginnings of human literacy. It is probably correct to say, as one writer has done, that "history begins at Sumer," for history, narrowly speaking, is the reconstruction of the past from written sources, and our first strictly historical evidence is Sumerian. The writing consists of wedge-shaped marks inscribed on clay tablets with a reed stylus, a technique that long persisted in Mesopotamia and spread throughout much of the Near East.* The script is called *cuneiform* after the Latin *cuneus,* "wedge." The first cuneiform symbols were pictograms, that is, little pictures of the objects being described. In time, the pictograms evolved into ideograms (conventionalized figures representing things or abstract concepts: for example, & for *and*). And scribes gradually achieved greater flexibility by adding syllabic symbols (representing phonetic values). Since the cuneiform symbols were exceedingly numerous, writing was a difficult and esoteric art that remained for many centuries the monopoly of a small, highly trained scribal class.

Sumerian mathematics seems to have arisen also from the necessities of the temple accounts. Ten was the basic numerical unit among the Sumerians as among many other peoples, perhaps because the decimal system is based on the primitive impulse to count on one's fingers. But the Sumerians also stressed units based on the numbers 6, 60, 600, 3600, and so on, which are the source of our practice of dividing circles into 360°. They understood addition and subtraction, and knew how to

---

*The earliest inscribed tablets thus far discovered are from the Sumerian city of Uruk and date back to around 3500 B.C. (above, p. 11).

handle fractions. They established standard units of weight and measure and perfected a lunar calendar. All these achievements were the products of hard, practical necessity, and all appear to have risen first from the needs of the temple community. All, in short, were undertaken for the purpose of better serving the gods.

The invention of writing was followed by the birth of literature. Here, too, the gods played a dominant role. The tragic and powerful *Epic of Gilgamesh* describes a Sumerian hero's courageous but fruitless search for immortality and includes an early version of the flood legend. Rich in hymns, prayers, and mythological poetry, Sumerian literature is characterized by a grave, solemn style that scarcely changed at all from one generation to the next. Sumerian authors and poets saw no value in originality but preferred to follow earlier models and preserve a cherished tradition.

Many of these same qualities affected Sumerian sculpture. It too was almost exclusively religious, and much of it was devoted to the decoration of the temples. It was executed in a style that by modern standards seems static, somber, and impersonal, and despite a gradual trend toward realism it was nearly as tradition-bound as literature. Yet the statuettes and relief carvings of the Sumerian artists also convey a feeling of dignity and nobility. Altogether they constitute a moving expression of the Sumerian religious outlook and take their place alongside the works of the poets and architects as the first expressions of a cultural tradition that was to dominate Western Asia for thousands of years.

MESOPOTAMIAN CHRONOLOGY (ALL DATES B.C. AND APPROXIMATE)

8,000–4,000	Neolithic era
4,000–2350	Civilization emerges; intercity warfare
2400–2250	Ebla flourishes
2370–2200	Akkadian Empire: Dynasty of Sargon
2100–2000	Empire of Ur: the Sumerians' Last Hurrah
2000–1530	Amorite domination: Old Babylonian Empire
1700–1500	Emergence of Indo-European peoples
1700	Code of Hammurabi
1530–1100	Kassites dominate Mesopotamia

Figure from Sumerian Temple about 3000 B.C. (*The Metropolitan Museum of Art, Fletcher Fund, 1940*).

EARLY SUMERIAN POLITICS

Sumerian society was characterized by a male-dominated hierarchy of priests, nobles, free workers, and peasants. The peasants, who far outnumbered everyone else, were obliged to work the temple lands or the lands of nobles, but they were also given the opportunity to till their own fields and to sell their own surpluses (if any). They were "slaves," to be sure, but slaves of the gods, and they shared this status with all ranks of society, even nobles and priests. And if all were slaves of the gods then, in at least some sense, all were equal. Indeed, most of the Sumerian cities first appear to have been governed by a general assembly of adult males. The practice quickly developed, however, of appointing a temporary king to rule during emergencies.

In time, emergencies, actual or contrived, became more frequent until finally monarchy became permanent. The chief priest and the king were often the same person, for Sumerian kingship, like almost every other Sumerian institution, was primarily religious in its function. It was the king's task to determine the gods' will by means of dreams or other portents and to carry it out. Even this mighty personage was merely the foremost slave of the city's chief god.

During the third millennium numerous city-states occupied the valley, bearing such poetic names as Ur, Lagash, and Uruk. The increasing frequency of emergencies and the concomitant rise of monarchies stemmed largely from the growing tendency toward intercity warfare. The ultimate political unification of the district was long delayed by the fierce independence of the cities. Prisoners taken in the intensified warfare of the epoch became the nucleus of a growing class of enslaved laborers, which had been inconsequential during Mesopotamia's early days.

As the struggles went on, Sumerian civilization spread northward along the Tigris-Euphrates Valley into a district called Akkad. This region was settled chiefly by Semitic-speaking peoples who had migrated from their original homeland in the Arabian Desert northward into Syria and then eastward into Mesopotamia. The inhabitants of Akkad built cities of their own and joined in the intercity battles. Thenceforth Mesopotamia was divided between the Semitic northern district of Akkad and the Sumerian south, usually called Sumer. But the relationships between Semites and Sumerians were exceedingly complex, and we must not view these peoples simply as two antagonistic blocs. Occasionally, during the third millennium, a single city would succeed in dominating all Mesopotamia, but its success was usually fleeting. Sometimes a Sumerian city would gain the ascendancy, sometimes an Akkadian city. And there is evidence that portions of Mesopotamia fell for a time under the control of external peoples.

CONTACTS TO THE EAST AND WEST

As Mesopotamian civilization developed, it came into contact with city-states that were emerging far to the east and west of the Tigris-Euphrates Valley. The previously mentioned Neolithic village of Tepe Yahya in Iran, some 500 miles to the east of Mesopotamia, had evolved by about 3400 B.C. into a city-state whose scribes were recording commercial transactions on clay tablets. Tepe Yahya grew much larger after about 3200 B.C., by which time other Iranian cities were also keeping written records. The scribes at Tepe Yahya, as elsewhere in Iran, inscribed their tablets in a language altogether different from that of Mesopotamia: they wrote in the earliest-known form of old Iranian. Tepe Yahya may well have been one of several way stations in a little-known commercial network linking Mesopotamia to the Indus Valley. But the Iranian discoveries are relatively recent and their full implications remain to be worked out.

Still more recently, in 1975, a team of Italian archeologists announced the discovery of a great city called Ebla, far to the west of Mesopotamia in northern Syria. In the "Palace of Ebla" they found many thousands of clay tablets, the earliest dating back to about 2400 B.C. The tablets, only partially deciphered, are inscribed in Mesopotamian cuneiform script, but in a language that is not Sumerian but Semitic. The evidence suggests that Ebla (meaning perhaps "The City of the White Stones") was the center of a flourishing kingdom in the third millennium B.C.

and a potent military and commercial rival to the city-states of Mesopotamia. Ebla's trade network extended eastward past Mesopotamia into western Iran, and southward and westward into Palestine and Anatolia (Asia Minor, the modern Turkey). At its height, around 2400−2250 B.C., Ebla appears to have controlled a considerable empire encompassing northern Syria, lower Anatolia, and even for a time parts of northern Mesopotamia.

THE UNIFICATION OF MESOPOTAMIA

While Ebla flourished, the Akkadian conqueror Sargon (c. 2370−2315 B.C.) was bringing all of Mesopotamia under his dominion. Sargon made a deep impression on his contemporaries, for his empire was the first to bind Akkad and Sumer into a single, durable unit. Later legend extended his conquests still further. Sargon is said to have "reigned over the people of all lands," though in fact, as we now know, he had to share the Near Eastern stage with the empire of Ebla.

Sargon's descendants maintained uneasy control for several generations. Around 2250 B.C. his grandson settled the Near Eastern power struggle by leading an army into Syria and burning Ebla to the ground. And some of Sargon's successors, breaking with Mesopotamian tradition, took the step of claiming divinity for themselves.

In time Sargon's Akkadian dynasty was destroyed by invaders from the northeast, whose coming brought another period of political upheaval. Around 2100 B.C., the Sumerian city of Ur rose to dominance (and its kings likewise claimed divinity). But after a century of fame and fortune, the empire of Ur fell victim to local particularism and invasions from Iran. With its collapse Sumerian political power was ended forever.

During the troubled era around 2000 B.C., several new Semitic peoples were moving into the valley. One such group, the Amorites from Syria, occupied a number of Mesopotamian cities, including the obscure community of Babylon. In time the Amorites widened their dominion and Babylon evolved into a great imperial capital. Hammurabi (c. 1700B.C.), the most celebrated of the Amorite kings of Babylon, conquered all of Akkad

Model of city of Ur, about 2000 B.C. (courtesy of the American Museum of Natural History).

and Sumer and eventually extended his sway across the entire Fertile Crescent from the Mediterranean Sea to the Persian Gulf.

The evidence for these political developments is thin and ambiguous, and certain details of our reconstruction may be in error. Our dates in this early period may be inexact by a century or more. Nevertheless, the general sequence of events is well established. And it seems clear enough that Hammurabi, building on a Sumerian cultural tradition that had been evolving for nearly 2000 years, was able to create a political structure of exceptional efficiency. His well-known law code, engraved on an eight-foot pillar, provides us with a window into daily life in the Babylonian Empire.

The code was based on a series of earlier, shorter Sumerian codes and drew heavily from Sumerian custom. Hammurabi makes no claim to personal divinity but assumes the more traditional role of steward of the gods. The society that he rules is stratified into nobles, free workers, and slaves. Detailed mercantile regulations indicate an active, complex commercial life. But the Code of Hammurabi is harsher than its Sumerian predecessors, suggesting a higher degree of authoritarianism than before. Capital punishment is frequent where it had once been rare, and the notion of retributive justice—an eye for an eye—is carried to macabre extremes: if a house collapses, killing its occupant, the builder is executed; if the occupant's son is killed, the builder's son must die; if a patient dies during an operation, the surgeon is executed; if the patient loses an eye, the surgeon loses his fingers—and with them, one presumes, his career.

THE EMERGENCE OF INDO-EUROPEAN PEOPLES: c. 1700–1500 B.C.

Even as the Babylonian Empire was at its height, new peoples were moving into the civilized districts of the Fertile Crescent from the surrounding mountains and deserts. They are known collectively as Indo-Europeans, for although they were ethnically diverse, their languages were all derived from a single Indo-European core—the ancestor of Latin, Greek, Persian, Sanskrit, and the Romance and Germanic languages of today

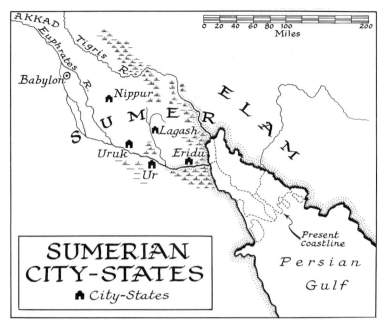

Sumerian City-States.

(including, of course, English). From the standpoint of language, these newcomers were our own forebears. Between about 1700 and 1500 B.C. they, and others in their wake, disrupted the political and cultural continuity of the ancient Near East. Around 1530 Indo-European invaders from Iran, known as Kassites, brought an end to Hammurabi's dynasty in Babylon. Like other Indo-European peoples, the Kassites used horses and chariots to conquer and intimidate. Kassite rulers managed to dominate Mesopotamia for the next four centuries—not as gods or as agents of gods, but simply as the lords of a landholding nobility that enjoyed a monopoly on chariots.

Before looking further at the Semitic and Indo-European kingdoms of western Asia, we will turn from the Tigris-Euphrates to the Valley of the Nile where another great civilization was developing.

Chapter
3

Egypt

THE SETTING

"Egypt is the gift of the Nile." It was the Greek historian Herodotus who made this observation, but its truth had long been recognized by the Egyptians themselves. One of their most moving hymns opens with these words: "Hail to thee, O Nile, that issues from the earth and comes to keep Egypt alive!"*

The Valley of the Nile winds northward like a green serpent through the barren North African desert, spreading as it approaches the Mediterranean into a vast flat delta. The narrow valley to the south and the delta to the north form two distinct regions known as Upper and Lower Egypt. (Since the two regions are named according to their location on the northward

---

*J. B. Pritchard, ed., *Ancient Near Eastern Texts* (Princeton, 1950), p. 372.

Mediterranean Sea

Nile Delta

Dead Sea

Canopus

Sais

Naukratis

Tanis

LOWER EGYPT

Heliopolis

GIZA PYRAMIDS

Saqqara

Memphis

LIBYA

SINAI PEN.

Herakleopolis

Hermopolis

Akhetaton

Lycopolis

W e s t e r n

Eastern

Red Sea

This

Abydos

Karnak

(Thebes)

Valley of The Kings

Western Thebes

Luxor

UPPER EGYPT

Desert

D e s e r t

Hierakonpolis

Ombos

Syene

Elephantine I.

Philae

1st cataract

Region of Fertility

Nile R.

2nd cataract

3rd cataract

N U B I A

4th cataract

ANCIENT
EGYPT

■ Capitals

Scale of Miles

0   50   100   200

flowing Nile, Lower Egypt will be *above* Upper Egypt on a modern map.) Ancient Egypt has thus been called "the Kingdom of the Two Lands."

UNIFICATION AND CULTURAL DEVELOPMENT: c. 3200–2600 B.C.

The remarkable fertility of the Nile Valley, like that of the Tigris-Euphrates, resulted from the rich silt deposited by annual floods. The evolution from Neolithic culture to civilization in Egypt followed the Mesopotamian pattern: swamps were drained, junglelike vegetation was cleared, and canals were dug, so that the fecundity of the black soil could be exploited. Indeed, the presence of Sumerian artifacts and artistic motifs from the beginning of this formative period suggests a Mesopotamian influence in Egypt's rise to civilization. An ancient Mesopotamian knife, for example, turned up in the Wadi Hammamat near the Nile, and the early Egyptian step pyramids bear a resemblance to Mesopotamian ziggurats.

Toward the close of the fourth millennium, the Nile Valley was divided into political units called nomes. Gradually these nomes coalesced into the two kingdoms of Upper and Lower Egypt, and around 3100 B.C. a half-legendary conqueror from Upper Egypt named Narmer (or Menes) unified the entire land. He established his capital at Memphis and became the first of the pharaohs.

The next 500 years constitute an ill-recorded but intensely creative epoch in Egyptian history. Between about 3100 and 2600 B.C., while the early pharaohs were consolidating their hereditary authority, a culture was developing that would shape Egyptian life for the next two millennia. The irrigation system was much expanded. An extensive knowledge of observational astronomy was put to use in the development of a 365-day solar calendar, far more accurate than the lunar calendar of the Mesopotamians. The early Egyptians did important work in physiology and medicine that would not be surpassed until the time of the Greeks. A graceful, majestic artistic style evolved, and architects were showing increasing skill in designing large structures of stone. Hieroglyphic writing, already known in 3100 B.C., developed into a literary vehicle. This was an exciting, adventurous period of artistic and cultural experimentation; at its close, in about 2600 B.C., Egyptian civilization had reached maturity. It is well to pause here to examine the culture that was taking form.

ENVIRONMENT AND OUTLOOK

Although both Egypt and Mesopotamia arose out of the taming of river valleys, the two civilizations differed sharply in style and mood, in part because they differed in environment. The Nile Valley was kinder to its inhabitants than was the Valley of the Two Rivers. The Nile floods might occasionally elude human control, and there were lean years in Egypt as well as abundant ones, yet, on the whole, the Egyptian environment was beneficient. The flooding Nile raged less savagely than the Tigris-Euphrates. The winds were softer and the sky clearer. In contrast to present-day Egypt, the population of the Nile Valley in antiquity was relatively small and the natural resources of the area were usually sufficient to support it. Finally, the surrounding deserts tended to protect Egyptian civilization, especially in its earlier phases, from the incessant invasions that afflicted Mesopotamia. There was an amiable regularity to life in ancient Egypt, and the forces of nature seemed friendlier and less menacing.

Accordingly, the ancient Egyptians tended to be confident, pragmatic, and optimistic. They were convinced that nature had blessed them and would continue to do so—that they were a singularly favored people. Above all, they possessed a sense of security lacking among the Mesopotamians. Of course individuals differ, and early Egypt doubtless had its pessimists just as Mesopotamia had its optimists, but the mood expressed by early Egyptian art, architecture, and literature is one of serenity and confidence—often even joy and exuberance. The emphasis is on material values—on the good things of this world and the pleasures of the moment.

Once established, Egyptian culture and Egyptian society

changed little over the centuries. This conservatism was by no means absolute, for the Egyptian spirit was sufficiently tolerant and undogmatic to accept such cultural adjustments as changing conditions might require. Yet by the standards of later civilizations, Egypt was remarkably static. Its inertia was in part a product of its isolation but stemmed also from the attitude of the Egyptians themselves. Theirs seemed the best of all possible worlds, and their impulse was to perpetuate rather than change it. They hoped, indeed they confidently expected, that the future would be an endless extension of the present.

The Egyptian preoccupation with the afterlife, often regarded as morbid, seems actually to have been a variation on this same theme—a bold assertion that the basic realities of the present would last forever in both this world and the next. It was not an obsession with death but a confident affirmation of life.

MA'AT AND THE PHARAOH

The Egyptians responded to nature's favor by viewing the universe as orderly and benevolent. The key concept in Egyptian religious thought is expressed in the word *ma'at*, which can be translated variously as "truth," "justice," "harmony," "balance," or "righteousness." The gods were not ferocious and arbitrary as in Mesopotamia, nor were the Egyptians their slaves. On the contrary, the gods cared about Egypt and favored it exceedingly. Indeed, the pharaoh himself was a living god and his rule was, at least ideally, a manifestation of *ma'at*. All Egypt was his personal estate, and his whim was law. Egypt produced no law codes as Mesopotamia did, for the law was in the pharaoh's mouth. Yet, being a god, he expressed in his words and deeds the basic harmony of the cosmos. He was the victorious champion of the Egyptians against the forces of chaos and darkness.

The potency of the god-king concept affected every aspect of ancient Egyptian life. The great early works of monumental architecture were royal tombs rather than temples—although temple architecture became significant in the later phases of the civilization. Most of the early sculpture and decorative art was associated with the tombs of the pharaohs. All Egyptians were subject to the pharaoh's orders. All gave large portions of their produce to the royal treasury and could be drafted to work on the royal tombs or in the royal mines. The pharaoh possessed a monopoly on foreign trade, and controlled much of the Egyptian economy.

Yet this king-centered system did not break the spirit of the individual Egyptian. Peasants are shown in the tomb scenes singing at their work. There was opportunity for people of ability to rise and prosper in the pharaoh's service. It is perhaps going too far to suggest, as one enthusiastic scholar has done, that the pyramids themselves were vast public works projects. But one does get the impression that the rule of the god-king was accepted gratefully, not sullenly; Egyptian history is almost entirely free of lower-class rebellions.

RELIGIOUS THOUGHT

Like other ancient peoples, the Egyptians crowded their universe with gods and spirits. Their greatest god, Re, personified the life-giving sun. He appeared in many guises and was often merged with some local god into a kind of divine compound. Amon-Re became in middle and later Egyptian history the most illustrious of these compound gods. During the imperial period, Amon-Re was god of victories and his magnificent temple at Karnak became unimaginably wealthy.

Osiris, another important deity, was said to have once been a benevolent pharaoh who taught his people agriculture. His sister-wife Isis, symbolic of the fertile earth, was believed to have been supremely wise and adept at the arts of magic. Later legend declared that Osiris had been killed by Set, his animal-headed brother but, owing to the lamentations of Isis, was miraculously resurrected. Osiris afterwards passed on into the next world to become the judge of souls.

This theme of death and resurrection was basic to ancient religious thought. A mythological expression of the death of vegetation in winter and its resurrection in spring, the concept also symbolized the death of the sun each evening and its rebirth at dawn. Indeed, the Nile itself followed this same sequence; the low Nile of early spring, bringing the specter of famine to the land, gave way each summer to a new, resurgent Nile that revivified the fields. And individual Egyptians might well hope that they too, like the sun and the river, would conquer death. The Osiris-Isis myth eventually came to symbolize this hope of individual salvation and eternal life. It remained an important mystery cult in Hellenistic and Roman times.

The pharaoh himself was identified with the god Horus, the son of Isis and Osiris, but he also claimed to be the son of Re. This illogical situation is typical of Egyptian religious thought which was a luxuriant tangle of incongruities. They were accepted cheerfully by the tolerant Egyptian, whose religious orientation was mythological and poetic rather than systematic.

EGYPTIAN CHRONOLOGY

Approximate Dates B.C.

3100	Traditional date of Menes' unification of Egypt
3100–2600	Early Dynastic Period
2600–2150	Old Kingdom (Pyramid Era: 2550–2400)
2150–2040	First Intermediate Period
2040–1650	Middle Kingdom
1650–1567	Second Intermediate Period: Era of the Hyksos
1567–1069	New Kingdom (Akhenaten: 1367–1350)

THE OLD KINGDOM: c. 2600–2150 B.C.

The coming of age of Egyptian civilization was followed by a 450-year period known as the Old Kingdom during which Egyptian culture flourished under the power of the pharaohs and the favor of the gods. The Old Kingdom was Egypt's classical age. At no other time was Egypt so stable or so confident.

The authority and prestige of the pharaohs of this period are illustrated dramatically by the pyramids in which they were entombed, the largest of which were built during the fourth

Model of Great Pyramid complex (*The Metropolitan Museum of Art, Dodge Fund, 1911*).

dynasty (c. 2550–2400). The Great Pyramid of Khufu (or Cheops: about 2500) is an immense mass of more than six million tons of stone fitted together with the precision of a watchmaker—a testimony not only to the skill and patience of its builders but also to their knowledge of practical mathematics. The pyramids were built without tackle, pulleys, cranes, or wheeled vehicles (the wheel had not yet come to Egypt). The cost in human labor must have been prodigious, yet we need not regard the pyramids as brutal monuments to the royal ego. As god-king, the pharaoh was the nexus of Egyptian religious thought, and his tomb was a kind of national religious monument. The proper entombment of the dead pharaoh was essential, so it was believed, to the perpetuation of *ma'at* and the continued prosperity of the kingdom.

THE FIRST INTERMEDIATE PERIOD: c. 2150–2040 B.C.

As the Old Kingdom drew to its end, the power and majesty of the pharaoh began to wane while the status of the priesthood and nobility rose. The *nomarchs*, who served as the pharaoh's agents in the provinces or nomes, became increasingly autonomous, and their offices evolved into hereditary lordships. Around 2150 the authority of the pharaoh was eclipsed altogether, and the nomarchs became the real masters of the land. The era of unrest and particularism that followed is known as the First Intermediate Period. The breakdown was purely internal, brought about by excessive delegation of royal rights and by the ever-increasing burden of building and maintaining the stupendous royal tombs. Egypt's isolation continued to shelter her from external dangers; like the imaginary kingdom of Oz, the Egyptian monarchy was protected by a deadly desert from every threat except that of the nomes.

The collapse of royal authority with its concomitant social upheaval was a devastating blow to Egyptian confidence. Writers of the age bemoaned the loss of *ma'at*. Some pondered the advantages of suicide; others lost themselves in wine, women, and song. One writer complains, "I show you the land topsy-turvy. That which never happened has happened. Men take up weapons of warfare, so that the land lives in confusion . . ."*

But the general Egyptian reaction to this disaster was neither cynicism nor despair. It was a serious effort to replace the old materialistic values of the past with deeper spiritual and moral values. Eternal life had formerly been associated with huge tombs and limited to the pharaoh and his immediate followers. Now salvation was made to depend more upon an upright life than an appropriate tomb, and the possibility of an afterlife was extended to nobles and commoners. Eternity was democratized.

This new cosmic egalitarianism affected Egyptian thought and society in a hundred different ways. A text from the First Intermediate Period has the creator god say, "I made the four winds that every man might breathe thereof . . . I made the great inundation that the poor man might have rights therein like the great man . . . I made every man like his fellow."† For the first time 'in human history, long before the age of the socially conscious Hebrew prophets, Egypt glimpsed the doctrine of human dignity and justice for the individual. The rulers of society were urged to treat their people righteously or else forfeit eternal life.

THE MIDDLE KINGDOM: c. 2040–1650 B.C.

Gradually, the Egyptian monarchy recovered something of its former position, and with this revival of centralized authority the Middle Kingdom began. The pharaohs now ruled from Thebes in Upper Egypt. Under their direction, Egypt's confidence and sense of special election returned. The doctrine of the god-king persisted. Even the old materialism and optimism reemerged, but they were tempered by the social conscience that Egypt had newly acquired. From our own viewpoint it is one of the tragedies of Egyptian history that as the Middle Kingdom prospered the impulse toward a recognition of human

---

*Quoted in John A. Wilson, *The Culture of Ancient Egypt* (Chicago, 1951), p. 107.
†*Ibid.*, p. 117.

dignity gradually waned and finally disappeared. The vision was daring and unprecedented, but did not last.

Nor did the monarchy rule with its former absolute authority. The nomarchs remained powerful, and the priesthood grew richer and stronger. But art and literature flourished once more, always within the framework of ideas and forms established during the first dynasties. Egyptian cultural influences and commercial relationships now spread far beyond the Nile valley —southward into the Sudan and northward into Palestine and Syria. And the tomb scenes show the same gaiety and humor as before.

THE SECOND INTERMEDIATE PERIOD: c. 1650–1567 B.C.

At about the time that various Indo-European peoples were disrupting Mesopotamia, a group known as the Hyksos was settling in Egypt. The Hyksos were a mixture of various peoples, largely Semitic in language and culture. Where they came from nobody knows, but somewhere they had encountered and adopted the new military technology, as yet unknown to the Egyptians, of horse-drawn chariots and improved bronze weapons. Encouraged by renewed internal tensions during the closing years of the Middle Kingdom, the Hyksos used their military edge to take over the Egyptian government and hold it for nearly a century. Their victory marked the beginning of a Second Intermediate Period (c. 1650–1567).

Although the influence of the Hyksos in Egyptian life was limited chiefly to the collection of tribute, they diminished the feeling of confidence and buoyancy that Egypt's former isolation had fostered. The continuity of Egyptian culture was by no means ended, but it was compromised. Thereafter, Egypt was never quite the same.

THE NEW KINGDOM: c. 1567–1069 B.C.

In time the Egyptians learned from their new masters about horses and chariots and, around 1567 B.C., used them to oust the

Hyksos from power. Then for a third time the monarchy asserted itself, and the New Kingdom came into being.

After about a century of consolidation, the pharaohs began to pursue a policy of imperialism, leading large armies out of a land that had once known only small police forces and milita. The Egyptians quickly extended their military and commercial influence over an extensive region that included the rich provinces of Syria and Palestine. Egypt's age of innocence was over at last, and the Valley of the Nile was now open not only to new luxuries but also to new styles, new ideas, and new religions.

The intellectual and artistic currents of this cosmopolitan age wrought a violent transformation in the Egyptian mood. The old serenity gave way to an exciting, fluid, occasionally nervous style. The old idealized portraiture evolved into extreme realism, even caricature and an obsession with the grotesque. The newly expanded kingdom maintained itself only at the cost of constant watchfulness and ever-increasing tension, and the old sense of confidence and optimism, shattered by the Hyksos, did not return. The social conscience of the First Intermediate Period and early Middle Kingdom was beyond recovery in the regimented society that the burden of imperialism made necessary. Yet despite the new regimentation and sharp social stratification, the pharaoh was no longer the divine autocrat that the Old Kingdom had known. His independence and authority were increasingly compromised by the rise of priestly power, and his wealth was rivaled by that of the god Amon-Re.

AKHENATEN: c. 1367−1360 B.C.

Etched against this fluctuating background is the tragic figure of the pharaoh Akhenaten, who has been described as humanity's first monotheist. Akhenaten rejected the many gods whom Egyptians had habitually worshipped. He defied the powerful priesthood of Amon-Re, suppressed the cult of Osiris, and effaced the names of these and other gods from the temples. In their place Akhenaten established a new god, the Aten, who is represented in the art of the period by a solar disc with rays extending outward ending in hands. The Aten was the god of the universe, the ultimate source of *ma'at*, the creator of the world. Akhenaten declared in his hymn to the Aten:

O sole god, like whom there is no other!
Thou didst create the world according to thy desire,
*Whilst thou wert alone.**

Akhenaten's theological revolution was an outgrowth of the new imperial age. For one thing, it was an attempt to destroy the ever-increasing power of the established priesthoods, especially that of Amon-Re. For another, the Aten's universality reflects the new cosmopolitanism of a people whose world was no longer bounded by the Valley of the Nile. And in the art associated with Akhenaten and his court, the fluid, realistic style of the New Kingdom reached a crescendo. Yet Akhenaten was himself no imperialist; Egypt's influence in foreign lands was allowed to crumble during his reign and had to be rebuilt by his successors.

The worship of the Aten scarcely survived Akhenaten's death, although the new artistic tendencies continued to flourish. Within a few years the bold heresy had been demolished, and Osiris and Amon-Re returned in triumph. Why did Akhenaten fail? Doubtless there were many reasons, but perhaps the most significant is the nature of the Aten itself. It was a cold and distant deity, a god of the intellect rather than the emotions. Nor was it really the only god, for Akhenaten, following Egyptian tradition, regarded himself as divine. Indeed, in his system only the pharaoh and his family worshipped the Aten. Everybody else worshipped the pharaoh. "Thou art in my heart," said Akhenaten to his god, "And there is no other that knows thee."** Consequently the Aten had no real impact on Egypt at large even during Akhenaten's reign. The theory that Akhenaten's religious ideas influenced the Hebrews who were then slaves in Egypt, thereby propelling Israel toward monotheism, seems most unlikely. But whatever its weak-

---

*Tr. J. A. Wilson, in J. B. Pritchard, ed., *The Ancient Near East* (Princeton, 1958), p. 229.

**Ibid.*, p. 230.

Akhenaten, with his wife Nefertiti behind him, worshipping the Aten
(*Art Reference Bureau—Cairo Museum*).

nesses, Akhenaten's vision was of singular nobility and breadth. If he fell short of monotheism, he approached it more closely than anyone before him.

CONCLUSION

The empire, which survived Akhenaten's death by nearly three centuries, ultimately succumbed to disintegration from within and attacks from without. Thereafter Eygpt was ruled for the most part by foreign dynasties or foreign peoples—Libyan, Assyrian, Persian, Greek, and Roman. During the intervals between these periods of foreign domination the Egyptians sought to recapture their earlier creative spirit, but it always eluded them. The forms of the past were repeated endlessly but the spirit of the past was beyond recovery.

Egyptian civilization ended ingloriously, as perhaps all civilizations must, but it had remained vigorous for two thousand years. The Egyptians failed to achieve eternity as they had hoped, but they came closer to doing so than any other people. And although their dynamism was exhausted at last, their art and architecture, their science and medicine, even their religion, became the legacy of newer cultures. The Greek column is Egyptian in origin, and the Greeks were honest enough to admit their debt to Egypt in science, medicine, and mathematics. Above all, the Egyptians, together with the Sumerians, were the creators of civilization itself. Israel and Persia, Greece and Rome, rose from their ruins.

Chapter
4

The Diffusion of Near Eastern Civilization

THE COMING OF THE IRON AGE

In the years following 1200 B.C., the civilizations of the ancient Near East were slowly transformed by the development and spread of iron smelting. As iron came more and more to replace bronze in the making of tools and weapons, the Bronze Age ended and the Iron Age began.

Well before 1200, iron technology seems to have been known to the Hittites, an Indo-European people that established a kingdom in Asia Minor (Turkey) around 1700 B.C. and reached the peak of their power in the fourteenth century. While the Pharaoh Akhenaten was offering devotions to the solar disc and challenging the priests of Amon-Re, the Hittites extended their power over Syria and Palestine at Egyptian expense. And when, a century later, the Pharaoh Ramses II launched a military campaign against Hittite Syria (c. 1265), the Hittites drove his army homeward and forced him to accept a treaty of "good peace and good brotherhood," sealed by a dynastic marriage. Then, around 1200, the Hittite kingdom was shattered forever by the onslaught of other Indo-Europeans of uncertain origin.

The Hittite kings had kept their iron technology a tightly guarded monopoly, but after 1200 B.C. iron tools and weapons spread across the ancient world. Iron smelting is more complicated than bronze smelting, but once the technique was understood iron came into widespread use. Not only was it harder and more durable than bronze, but far more abundant as well. The much increased availability of metal that resulted from this "iron revolution" had a distinctly democratizing effect. Bronze Age aristocracies lost their monopoly on metal as iron weapons and tools passed more and more into the hands of commoners.

THE CANAANITES

The collapse of the Hittites, and the concurrent decline of the Egyptian New Kingdom, presented a unique opportunity to the Semitic tribes of Syria and Palestine whose lands had hitherto been an imperial battleground. Indeed, the entire period from about 1200 to 750 B.C. was an interlude between imperial eras. The Hittites were crushed, Egypt and Mesopotamia dozed, and the great Near Eastern empires of Assyria and Persia lay off in the unknown future. In the interim, the peoples of the eastern Mediterranean shore found their place in the sun.

The dominant people in Syria-Palestine around the middle of the second millennium were known as Canaanites. The culture of their independent city-states, with its roots in both Mesopotamia and Egypt, was generally derivative. But they made one original contribution of tremendous significance: the development of the first true alphabet. In place of the hundreds of syllabic signs of the earlier scripts, the Canaanites used twenty-nine symbols representing the consonants. The alphabet was reduced later on to twenty-two letters, and still later the Greeks added vowels. But even without these improvements the Canaanite alphabet constituted an enormous simplification and opened up the possibility of a vast expansion of literacy. Writing was never again the mysterious art that it had formerly been, and the monopoly of the old scribal class was doomed. Like the coming of iron, the invention of the alphabet extended the benefits of civilization to a much larger segment of society than ever before.

The city-states of the Canaanites were subjected to violent attacks between 1300 and 1000. First came the Israelites who had crossed the Sinai Desert from Egypt. The next invaders were the Philistines, whom some scholars have associated with the group of "sea peoples" that invaded the New Kingdom of Egypt around 1200 B.C. The Canaanites lost most of their cities to the Israelites and Philistines (after whom "Palestine" is named), but managed to maintain control of a narrow coastal strip known as Phoenicia.

The Phoenicians, as these later Canaanites were called, had a remarkable talent for commerce. Independent Phoenician cities, such as Sidon and Tyre, sent their ships throughout the Mediterranean, transmitting Near Eastern goods and ideas into Europe and North Africa. The Greek language, for example, is written in an alphabet adapted from the Phoenician.

Merchants sailing westward from Phoenicia passed through the "Pillars of Hercules" (the later Straits of Gibraltar) and out into the Atlantic. They may well have reached Britain and the Azores, and they made their way southward down the west coast of Africa to Cape Verde. The greatest of the many Phoenician trading bases was Carthage in the western Mediterranean, founded by Tyre late in the eighth century and destined to acquire wealth and power far beyond the dreams of the Phoenicians themselves.*

THE ISRAELITES

No other ancient Near Eastern people are as familiar to us as the Israelites. The Bible has been studied by scholars and believers

---

*See pp. 151, 159.

throughout the centuries of Western Civilization. It is the fountainhead of Judaism, Islam, and Christianity, and a crucial element in the heritage of countless millions of people today. As an historical source it enables us to endow the dry bones of ancient Israel with flesh and life. But it also raises serious problems of historical criticism.

Biblical critics of the nineteenth century rejected the traditional belief in divine inspiration and subjected the Bible to painstaking scrutiny of the sort that historians normally apply to their documents. These critics doubted the historical existence of Abraham, Jacob—even Moses—and concluded that the Bible was not especially good history. More recently, however, Biblical episodes that were previously rejected as mere myth have been corroborated by new archeological discoveries and by comparisons with non-Biblical sources. Scholars are now inclined to regard the Bible as a relatively reliable body of ancient historical documents.

According to the Bible, the history of the Jews begins when the patriarch Abraham entered into an agreement or *Covenant* with a specific deity, "the God of Abraham." Abraham promised not to recognize or worship any other god, and, in return, he and his family were taken under the special protection of the God of Abraham. The Covenant was renewed by all succeeding generations of Abraham's clan and became a basic ingredient of Jewish religious thought. It seems unlikely that Abraham viewed his god as the only god. Had he been asked, he would probably have conceded the existence of other deities, yet from the *practical* standpoint even Abraham was a monotheist. The existence of other gods was irrelevant to him, for it was his god alone that Abraham honored.

Biblical evidence suggests that the first Hebrews came from Mesopotamia: the creation account, the Garden of Eden, and the Flood all seem to echo Mesopotamian traditions, and the biblical Tower of Babel may have been inspired by a ziggurat. Around 1500, perhaps in the wake of the Kassite invasion of Mesopotamia, the Hebrews migrated to Palestine and then, striken by famine, onward into Egypt. Abraham himself may well have led his clan from Mesopotamia to Palestine, and the further migration to Egypt is said to have been led by Jacob,

Abraham's grandson. The Hebrews in Egypt were probably not limited to Jacob and his family but included kindred folk, and perhaps other Semitic people who had filtered earlier into the Nile Valley.

It was the policy of the Egyptian New Kingdom to enslave all foreigners (the lesson of the Hyksos was not soon forgotten). While performing forced labor for the pharaohs, the Hebrews extended their Covenant of Abraham to include greater numbers of oppressed people. In the meantime Egypt enriched itself from the profits of empire, and Akhenaten experimented with his solar religion. But the Hebrews, at the bottom of the Egyptian social order, were essentially unaffected.

At length, perhaps around 1300 B.C., a Hebrew, trained in the Egyptian bureaucracy and bearing the Egyptian name of Moses, led a band of his own and other enslaved peoples to freedom. For a long generation they wandered in the wilderness of the Sinai Desert. Under Moses' superb leadership they were forged into a unified people and the personal Covenant was transformed into a Covenant between God and the whole Hebrew nation. The God of Abraham was given the name "Yahweh" (traditionally translated as Jehovah but, according to Hebrew doctrine, never to be spoken). It is to this Sinai period that the Bible ascribes the divine dictation of the Ten Commandments.

Moses had promised to lead his people to the "promised land" of Canaan. But when the Hebrews emerged at last from the wilderness, Moses was dead, and a new generation had arisen. Under the leadership of Joshua the Hebrews entered Palestine, perhaps around the mid-1200s, and won a series of victories over Canaanite cities. The best known of Joshua's battles was fought at the ancient city of Jericho whose walls, we are told, came tumbling down. But the struggle with the Canaanites did not end with these initial battles. It continued with many ups and downs for another two centuries, during which the Hebrews were deeply influenced by Canaanite civilization. They adopted a Canaanite dialect and the Canaanite alphabet. Some even began to worship Canaanite gods, much to the chagrin of the orthodox. During these centuries the Hebrews were loosely organized into tribes under local military leaders known inappropriately as "judges." The epoch of the judges gave way at length to a unified monarchy which was made necessary by the increasing military pressure of a new tribe of invaders: the Philistines.

THE UNITED ISRAELITE KINGDOM AND ITS AFTERMATH

In about 1020 B.C. the priest Samuel anointed Saul, Israel's first king. Saul waged war against the Philistines with some success but was outshone by his able successor, David (c. 1000–960), who is said to have demonstrated his prowess even as a child by slaying the great Philistine, Goliath, with a slingshot. Under David and his son Solomon (960–922), Israel reached its political zenith. Their kingdom was the most powerful in the ancient history of Syria-Palestine, dominating the entire area and extending far inland toward the Euphrates. Phoenicia retained its independence only through a policy of submissive cooperation. This was the golden age that etched itself on Israel's imagination for all time to come—the age that for endless generations the Jews never despaired of recovering.

It was David's great hope to build a permanent, central temple for Yahweh in Jerusalem, a city that he had recently conquered, and under Solomon the temple was completed. In it was enshrined the Arc of the Covenant, containing the two stones bearing the original inscriptions of the Ten Commandments. Jerusalem itself became the cosmopolitan capital of a wealthy empire. Solomon surrounded himself with all the trappings of Near Eastern monarchy, from bureaucrats to concubines. But Solomon's subjects were obliged to pay for all this imperial glory with heavy taxes and forced labor, and many of them concluded that the price was too high. Upon Solomon's death (922 B.C.), Israelite separatism reasserted itself, and the kingdom broke into two halves: a large state to the north known thenceforth as Israel, and the smaller, more unified state of Judah to the south, centering on Jerusalem.

This political split brought an early end to Hebrew imperialism. And with the rise of new Near Eastern empires, the Hebrews lost their political independence. The first of the new empires, the Assyrian, exerted increasing military pressure

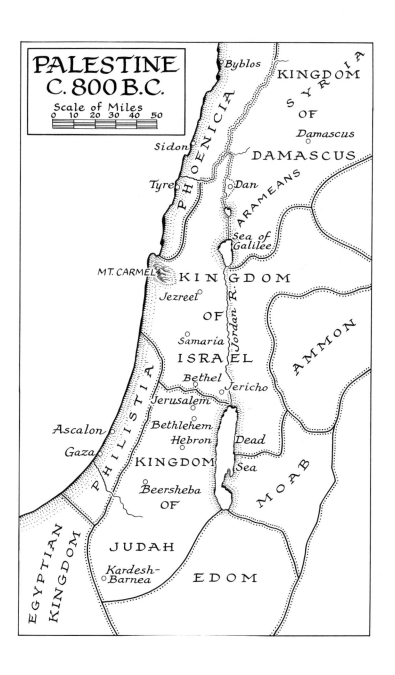

PALESTINE
C. 800 B.C.

Scale of Miles
0   10   20   30   40   50

Byblos

KINGDOM

S Y R I A

OF

Damascus

Sidon

DAMASCUS

Tyre

Dan

PHOENICIA

ARAMEANS

Sea of
Galilee

MT. CARMEL

KINGDOM

Jezreel

OF

Samaria

Jordan R.

AMMON

ISRAEL

Bethel

Jericho

Jerusalem

PHILISTIA

Bethlehem

Ascalon

Hebron

Dead

Gaza

KINGDOM

Sea

MOAB

Beersheba

OF

EGYPTIAN KINGDOM

JUDAH

Kardesh-
Barnea

EDOM

against both Israel and Judah. Israel fell to the Assyrians in 722, and its people were scattered across the Near East where they faded into the indigenous populations and vanished from history. They have been known ever since as the "ten lost tribes of Israel."

Judah survived the Assyrian attacks only to fall to Assyria's imperial successor, the New Babylonian Empire, in 586. Judah's political and intellectual leaders were banished to Babylon where they and their children endured that tragic epoch in Biblical history, the Babylonian Captivity (586–538 B.C.). The bitterness of exile is captured in the opening lines of the 137th Psalm:

By the rivers of Babylon,
There we sat down, yea, we wept,
*When we remembered Zion.**

THE PROPHETS

The devastating experience of divided kingdom and Babylonian Captivity evoked a profound religious response. During these years the moral initiative passed from kings and priests to inspired individuals known as prophets, whose spiritual insights—arising out of an age of despair—deepened and ennobled the Hebrew religion. To the prophets, law and ritual were insufficient without sincerity of purpose and righteousness of life. The prophet Micah expressed this idea with striking brevity:

It has been shown to you, O man, what is good
*   and what the Lord requires of you:*
Only to do justice
*   and live loyally*
*   and walk humbly with your God* [6:8].

---

*Originally, Zion was the name of the hill in Jerusalem on which Solomon's temple stood—the holy center of the Hebrew kingdom and faith. The term later acquired broader meanings: the Heavenly City; the people of Israel.

The teachings of the prophets were based on two fundamental concepts: (1) the Covenant between God and his Hebrew people, and (2) the consequent obligation of Israelites to treat one another justly. Their vision of justice and righteousness was not applied with any consistency to humanity at large but only to the Jewish community; yet even with that important qualification it was a profound affirmation of human dignity. Unlike the ephemeral social consciousness of the Egyptian Middle Kingdom, the prophetic teachings became a fundamental component of Hebrew thought. More than that, they underlie the tradition of social justice that has developed in Western Civilization. The prophets' insistence that all Israelites were equal in the sight of God would ultimately expand into the doctrine of universal human equality.

In the hands of the prophets, the concept of Yahweh was universalized. They explained the collapse of Solomon's empire and the Assyrian and Babylonian conquests by asserting that Yahweh had used the Hebrews' enemies to punish his chosen people for their transgressions and to prepare them for a triumphant future. But if this was so, then Yahweh's power was evidently not limited to the Hebrews but embraced all peoples. Whereas Yahweh had formerly been the only God that *mattered*, he was now proclaimed as the only God that *existed*. The prophet Amos quotes the Lord as saying,

Did I not bring up Israel
  from the land of Egypt
and the Philistines from Caphtor
  and the Syrians from Kir? [9:7]

Yahweh was the Lord of nations, yet the Hebrews remained his chosen people. History itself could be understood only in terms of Israel's encounter with God. The Hebrews were unique among the peoples of the ancient Near East in their sensitivity toward history, for to them God's relations with humanity occurred in a historical dimension, and history itself was directed by God toward certain predetermined goals. Thus, it was Yahweh, not the Babylonians, who sent the Hebrews into exile, and in the fullness of time, so the prophets said, Yahweh would build their kingdom anew. A divinely appointed leader of the house of David—a Messiah—would one day be sent to consummate the divine plan by reestablishing the political glory of Israel. This assurance helped the Hebrew exiles preserve their integrity and their faith against the lures of a powerful alien culture. For although many succumbed to the temptations of Babylon, others held fast in the conviction that history was on their side.

LATER JEWISH HISTORY

In 538 B.C. the New Babylonian Empire gave way to the Persian Empire, and the Hebrews were permitted to return to their homeland and rebuild the Temple of Jerusalem. They could now practice their faith without interference, but they remained under Persian political control. Two centuries thereafter Persian rule gave way to Greek rule, and in time the Greeks were replaced by the Romans. During these post-exilic centuries the Hebrews collected, sifted, and expanded their sacred writings, and the Old Testament acquired its final form.

As always, the Jews were torn between the desire to preserve the purity of their heritage and the impulse to accommodate themselves to outside cultural influences. From time to time they rebelled against their political masters but never with lasting success. A rebellion in A.D. 70 prompted the Romans to destroy their temple and scatter them throughout the Empire. There followed an exile far more prolonged than the earlier ones in Egypt and Babylonia, lasting until the present century. But the Jews had demonstrated long before that they could survive as a people and a faith without political unity.

The impact of the ancient Hebrews on future civilizations has been immense. The Old Testament, a tremendous literary monument in and of itself, has been of incalculable importance in the development of European culture. The Hebrews' sense of history—as a dynamic, purposeful, morally significant process of human-divine interaction—went far beyond the historical concepts of other Near Eastern peoples and became a fundamental element in the historical vision of Western Civilization. But at the core of everything is their ethical monotheism—their vision of a single God of infinite power who is also a God of righteousness and mercy. The Hebrews confronted their universe in a new way. The world was no longer pregnant with spirits; nature was no longer a "Thou," but rather the handiwork of a far greater "Thou." The myriad spooks and demons of tree, rock, and mountain dissolved before the unutterable holiness of the God of Israel.

THE NEW EMPIRES: ASSYRIANS AND CHALDEANS: c. 745–538 B.C.

The last phase of ancient Near Eastern history runs from the rise of the Assyrian Empire in the mid-eighth century B.C. to the conquest of the Persian Empire by the Greeks under Alexander the Great in 330 B.C. During these centuries Near Eastern imperialism reached its zenith.

The Assyrians, a Semitic people from northern Mesopotamia, had long been a power in the Near East. Following a policy of ruthless militarism, they created an empire that dominated Western Asia (745–612 B.C.) and for a time included Egypt as well. The entire ancient world was momentarily united under a power that terrorized its subjects and crushed insurrections with fearful severity. One Assyrian king boasted of punishing a group of rebels by tearing out their tongues, mashing them alive, and feeding their corpses to pigs and vultures.

Assyrian culture was Sumerian in inspiration. Its gods were similar to those of Sumer and Akkad although much more warlike. The Assyrian king, in good Sumerian tradition, was viewed as the human representative of the chief god, but his prestige was much higher than that of his Mesopotamian predecessors. The supreme expression of Assyrian architecture, for example, was the royal palace, not the temple.

Assyrian militarism brought unity and a degree of peace to the long-troubled Near East, but it was a peace based on terror. Once Assyrian leadership faltered, the Empire collapsed before the rage of its subject peoples. A coalition of Indo-European

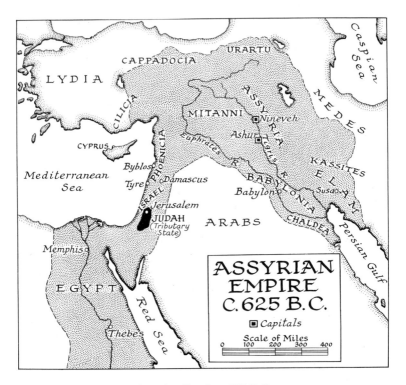

Assyrian Empire, 625 B.C.

Medes from Iran and Semitic Chaldeans from Babylonia de-stroyed the power of Assyria for all time to come. The Assyrian capital of Nineveh fell in 612 B.C., and its site remains desolate to this day.

Between the fall of Assyria and the rise of Persia (c. 612–538 B.C.) the Near East was divided among several powers. Egypt had already recovered its independence. Anatolia passed to the Lydians, a people who gave humanity its first real coinage and whose last king, Croesus, achieved fame as a monarch of legendary wealth. Assyria itself, together with the northern and eastern provinces of its former empire, became subject to the Medes. The southern and western provinces fell to the Chal-deans who established a New Babylonian Empire.

The Chaldeans rebuilt Babylon with unprecedented splendor

Lydian coins, 560 to 540 B.C. (*The American Museum of Art, Gift of the American Society for the Excavation of Sardis, 1926*).

in glazed, colored tiles decorated with fantastic animals. This was the age of Nebuchadnezzar and the Hebrew Babylonian Captivity. It was also the age of the "hanging gardens of Babylon" and the climax of Mesopotamian astrology. In their efforts to foretell the future and discern the wills of the gods, Chaldean wise men made painstaking observations of the stars and planets from observatories atop the towers of their fascinating city. This last brief Babylonian renaissance came to an end when the city fell to the Persians in 538.

THE PERSIAN EMPIRE: 538–330 B.C.

The Persians, like the Medes to whom they were closely related, were an Indo-European people settled on the Iranian plateau. Their traditional subordination to the Medes was reversed in 549 B.C. when the Persian leader, Cyrus the Great, seized the Medean crown and thenceforth ruled both peoples. During the subsequent decade Cyrus conducted an astonishing series of military campaigns which won him a wide empire stretching from India through Mesopotamia, Lydia, and Syria-Palestine, and earned him the greatest military reputation in the history of the ancient Near East. With the conquest and absorption of Egypt shortly after Cyrus' death, the Persians unified the entire Near East into a single empire.

The Persian Empire represents the synthesis of Near Eastern political and cultural traditions under a single government that achieved stability not through military terror but through toleration. The Jews returned to their homeland and rebuilt their

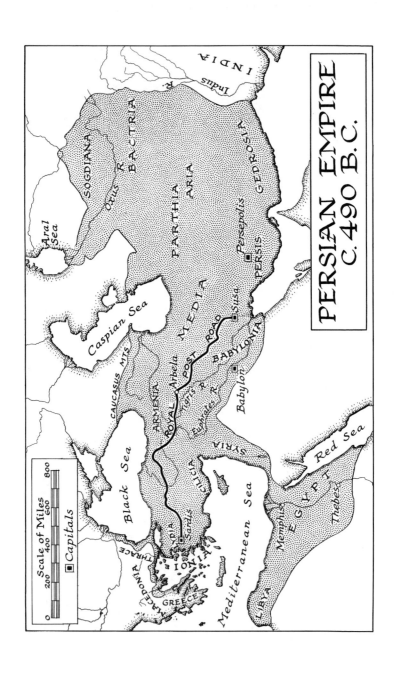

PERSIAN EMPIRE
C. 490 B.C.

Scale of Miles
0   200   400   600   800
■ Capitals

Aral Sea
SOGDIANA
Oxus R.
BACTRIA
Indus R.
INDIA
ARIA
PARTHIA
GEDROSIA
Persepolis
PERSIS
Susa
MEDIA
Caspian Sea
CAUCASUS MTS.
ARMENIA
Arbela
ROYAL POST ROAD
Tigris R.
BABYLONIA
Babylon
Euphrates R.
Black Sea
THRACE
MACEDONIA
LYDIA
Sardis
IONIA
GREECE
CILICIA
SYRIA
Mediterranean Sea
Red Sea
LIBYA
EGYPT
Memphis
Thebes

temple; all the peoples of the Empire were allowed a generous degree of religious and cultural autonomy.

The imperial administrative structure reached its fullest development under Darius the Great (521–486 B.C.). It consisted of an absolute hereditary monarchy assisted by a central council of nobles and represented in the imperial provinces by local governors called satraps. Although the various provinces were permitted to retain many of their individual customs, the monarchy kept close watch over them through a network of imperial inspectors who saw to it that the satraps remained both honest and loyal. Commerce was stimulated by an extensive network of roads and by the introduction of imperial coinage in the Lydian tradition. The Greek historian Herodotus commended the efficiency of the Persian postal service in these familiar words: "Neither snow nor rain nor heat nor gloom of night stays these couriers from the swift completion of their appointed rounds."

The culture of the Persian Empire is a summing up rather than a new departure. In most respects it is a development of age-old Mesopotamian concepts, although the use of tall stone columns gives Persian architecture a delicate elegance all its own. The Persian King of Kings, for all his imperial pomp, refrained from claiming divinity and was satisfied merely to stress his divine appointment.

It was in the religious sphere that the Persians showed their greatest originality. They, no less than the Jews, broke sharply with Near Eastern religious tradition. The almost legendary Persian prophet Zoroaster (or Zarathustra) proclaimed a highly intellectualized doctrine of ethical monotheism centering on the god Ahura Mazda (which means "the wise lord"). In the centuries after Zoroaster's death, the traditional Persian priesthood, the Magi, appropriated the doctrine and gradually altered it, incorporating older Iranian gods into the system as subordinate deities and elevating the evil god Ahriman to a position almost equal to that of Ahura Mazda. Zoroastrianism thus evolved into an intensely dualistic faith that stressed the universal struggle between good and evil. Ahura Mazda became the god of light, goodness, mind, and spirit; Ahriman represented darkness, evil, and matter. The material world and the human

Palace at Persepolis (Darius the Great). (*E. F. Schmidt, Persepolis I, OIP68, Pl. 50, Oriental Institute, University of Chicago.*)

body came to be viewed as evil; the spiritual world and the human soul as good. Zoroastrianism, alone among ancient Near Eastern religions, transcended both the state and the people that gave it birth and became a universal faith. It remained dominant in Iran and Mesopotamia until the Islamic conquests of the seventh century A.D. and exerted a strong influence on Jewish, Hellenistic, Roman, and medieval religious thought.

The last century of Persian rule saw a failure of imperial leadership. The earlier policy of toleration gave way to repression, and political efficiency was replaced by corruption and civil strife. The consequent loss of confidence and alienation of subject peoples set the stage for the spectacular victories of Alexander the Great* that destroyed the Persian Empire in 330 B.C. and ended the age-long drama of the ancient Near East.

Although Near Eastern civilization collapsed politically in 330 it survived in spirit, influencing not only Alexander the Great himself but also the post-Alexandrian Hellenistic world, which witnessed a significant interplay of Greek and Oriental cultures. From the beginning Greece was profoundly indebted to the Near East which was the source of its alphabet, much of its mythology and architecture, and the beginnings of its technology and science. The Greeks developed this intellectual and cultural legacy in ways unimagined by their predecessors. One Greek writer emphasized the point with charming immodesty when he said, "Whatever the Greeks take over from foreigners, they transform it by making it something finer." Yet behind Greece and Rome lies the rich experience of the ancient Near East without which these later civilizations would be inconceivable.

---

*See Chapter 10.

Approximate Dates B.C.	Mesopotamia	Egypt	Israel	Near East in General
4000	Formation of city-states (4000 ff.)			
3000		First Dynasties (3100–2600)		
2500				Ebla flourishes (2400–2250)
2250	Akkadian Empire Dynasty of Sargon (2370–2200) Empire of Ur (2100–2000)	Old Kingdom (2600–2150) 1st Inter. Per. (2150–2040)		
2000	Old Babylonian Empire (2000–1530)	Middle Kingdom (2040–1650)		
1900				
1800				Emergence of Indo-Europeans (1700–1500)
1700				Hittites flourish (1700–1200)
1600		2nd Inter. Per.: Hyksos (1650–1567)		
1500	Kassites (1530–1100)	New Kingdom (1567–1069)		
1400		Akhenaten (1379–1361)	Bondage in Egypt (?1450–1300)	
1300			Moses and Sinai Period (?1300–1260)	

Date				
1200				Beginning of Iron Age (1200)
1100	Post-Empire Period (1069 ff.)		Era of Judges (1230–1020)	
1000			United Kingdom (1020–933)	
900			Political split: Israel and Judah (933–722)	
800	Assyrian Empire (745–612)			Assyrian Empire (745–612)
700		Temporary Assyrian Conquest (671)	Israel falls to Assyrians (722)	
600	New Babylonian Empire (Chaldeans) (612–538)	Persian Conquest (525)	Judah falls: Babylonian captivity (586–538)	Lydians (fl. 683–546) Medes (fl. 612–549)
500	Persian Empire (538–330)		Return to Palestine (538 ff.)	Chaldeans (fl.612–538) Persian Empire (538–330)
400				
300	Conquest by Alexander (330)	Conquest by Alexander (332)		Conquest by Alexander (332–330)

Suggested Readings

PREHISTORY

Two excellent surveys are Robert Braidwood, *Prehistoric Men* (8th ed., 1975), and Brian M. Fagan, *World Prehistory: A Brief Introduction* (1979).

Richard E. Leakey and Roger Lewin, *Origins* (1977). A survey of the Leakey family's recent East African discoveries relating to human origins.

James Mellaart, *The Neolithic of the Near East* (1976). Discusses recent archeological investigations of Neolithic villages.

THE ANCIENT NEAR EAST

Good general studies include Henri Frankfort, *The Birth of Civilization in the Near East* (1968); Henri Frankfort and others, *The Intellectual Adventure of Ancient Man* (1977); William W. Hallo and W.K. Simpson, *The Ancient Near East: A History* (1971); and Sabatino Moscati, *The Face of the Ancient Orient* (1962).

MESOPOTAMIA

Samuel N. Kramer, *History Begins at Sumer* (1959). Gracefully written and adept in its use of Sumerian writings. See also Kramer's more recent work, *The Sumerians* (1971).

A. Leo Oppenheim, *Ancient Mesopotamia* (rev. ed., 1977). Makes full use of recent scholarship and excavations; particularly full on the Assyrians.

Georges Roux, *Ancient Iraq* (rev. ed., 1976). A comprehensive account of ancient Mesopotamia that uses contemporary writings with great skill.

Original sources include *The Epic of Gilgamesh*, tr. N. K. Sandars; and James B. Prichard, tr., *Ancient Near Eastern Texts Relating to the Old Testament* (1969).

EGYPT

Two good introductory works are Alan Gardiner, *Egypt of the Pharaohs* (1961), and Cyril Aldred, *The Egyptians* (1961).

Christiane Desroches-Noblécourt, *Tutankhamen* (1976). Stunning illustrations recreate the world of the New Kingdom pharaoh whose treasure recently toured the United States.

William K. Simpson, tr., *The Literature of Ancient Egypt: An Anthology of Stories, Instructions, and Poetry* (1972).

Jon M. White, *Everyday Life in Ancient Egypt* (1967). A short, fascinating account.

John A. Wilson, *The Culture of Ancient Egypt* (1959). A pioneering work of interpretation, daring in its time, now widely accepted.

THE DIFFUSION OF NEAR EASTERN CIVILIZATION

R. Collins, *The Medes and Persians: Conquerors and Diplomats* (1974). A fine recent account.

R. Ghirshman, *Iran* (1978). A comprehensive study drawn from the most recent evidence.

J. Maqueen, *The Hittites and their Contemporaries in Asia Minor* (1975). A good, recent introduction to the subject.

M. Pearlman, *In the Footsteps of Moses* (1974). An evocative study of Moses and the Exodus from Egypt.

Giuseppe Riccioti, *The History of Israel* 2nd ed., (1958). A standard treatment, marked by scholarly rigor.

N.K. Sandars, *The Sea Peoples: Warriors of the Ancient Mediterranean, 1250–1150 B.C.* (1978). Stresses the ambiguity of the evidence and the danger of overinterpreting it.

J. Van Seters, *Abraham in History and Tradition* (1975). An astute and successful effort to disentangle history and legend.

James Wellard, *By the Waters of Babylon* (1972). A very readable work on ancient Babylon stressing the investigations of archeologists.

R.R. Wilson, *Genealogy and History in the Biblical World* (1977). On the historical significance of the Hebrew religious tradition.

PART
2
GREECE

Chapter
5

Crete, Mycenae, and the Dark Age

THE NEW WORLD OF THE ANCIENT AEGEAN

Homer's *Odyssey*, one of the supreme Greek epic poems, tells of the perils and adventures of the Greek chieftain Odysseus as he sailed home from the fall of Troy. As a tale of a hero's conquest of the terrors of the ocean, the *Odyssey* symbolizes a central quality of the Greek experience. For the Greeks were, above all, a seafaring people. Sailing out from their barren, mountainous homeland, they planted colonies far and wide and eventually dominated the commerce of the eastern Mediterranean. In the end they, like their mythical hero Odysseus, conquered the sea and gained fame and sorrow in the process.

The two great Homeric epics, the *Odyssey* and the *Iliad*, originated in the eighth century B.C. Both poems tell of the conclusion and aftermath of a half-legendary, long-ago war between the Greeks and the Trojans—a struggle that ended with the Greek conquest of Troy. The *Iliad* and *Odyssey* mark the dawn of written Greek literature, yet they hark back to a civilization far older.

Not much more than a century ago the Homeric epics and the Trojan War were seen merely as inspired fancy. The picture that emerges in Homer's poems of a highly developed civilization in the Peloponnesus, dominated by King Agamemnon of Mycenae, was thought to be a folk myth and nothing more. But during the 1870s and 1880s Heinrich Schliemann, a retired businessman and amateur archeologist, confounded the scholarly world by excavating Troy, Mycenae, and other Homeric sites, thereby giving reality to a supposedly imaginary civilization that had flourished some eight centuries before the golden age of Athens. Early in the present century, Sir Arthur Evans' excavations at Cnossus on the island of Crete produced evidence of a civilization resembling that of Mycenae on the Greek mainland, but even older and more splendid. In 1952 Michael Ventris deciphered the *Linear B* script used at Cnossus and several mainland sites. The work of Schliemann, Evans, Ventris, and other students of early Aegean culture has opened a new world to us, but the study of this first European civilization remains fluid and exciting, with old theories constantly being upended by new discoveries.

GREEK CHRONOLOGY

All Dates B.C.

c. 2000−1400	Minoan Civilization flourishes
c. 1580−1120	Mycenaean Civilization flourishes
c. 1200	Trojan War
c. 1200−1000	Emergence of Dorian Greeks
c. 1120−800	"Dark Age"
c. 750−550	Era of colonization
c. 650 ff.	Rise of tyrants
590s	Solon reforms Athenian laws
c. 582−507	Pythagoras
561−527	Pisistratus rules Athens

508	Cleisthenes reforms Athenian laws
490–479	Persian Wars
477	Delian League established
c. 460–429	Era of Pericles
454	Delian treasury moved to Athens
432	Parthenon completed
431–404	Peloponnesian War
469–399	Socrates
427–347	Plato
384–322	Aristotle
359–336	Reign of Philip of Macedon
338	Battle of Chaeronea: Philip establishes mastery over Greece
336–323	Reign of Alexander the Great
323 ff.	The Hellenistic Age

MINOAN CIVILIZATION

The civilization of ancient Crete has been called "Minoan" after the half-legendary King Minos of Cnossus.* It derived its technological and artistic skills from Mesopotamia, Egypt, and western Asia Minor but developed them in highly original ways. As early as the third millennium the Minoans were engaged in a vigorous trade with the Near East. Shortly after 2000 B.C. the great Minoan palaces were built. During the next six centuries these palaces were destroyed time and again by earthquakes but always rebuilt on a grander scale than before. The "palace period" between about 2000 and 1400 B.C., marks the apex of Minoan Civilization. The greatest monument of the age was the Palace of Cnossus, a magnificent rambling structure of several stories surrounding a central court. The palace contained storage rooms where tall jars of olive oil and wine were kept, a remarkably sophisticated plumbing and drainage system, and a pillared throne room of great splendor. Minoan Crete had several smaller palaces as well as numerous luxurious private townhouses and country mansions. Surprisingly, the palaces

---

*The name "Minos" is suspiciously similar to the names of other legendary founder-kings: Menes of Egypt, Mannus of Germany, Manu of India, and so on.

and towns of the Minoan golden age had no appreciable fortifications. Scenes of warfare in some recently discovered Minoan frescoes would seem to rule out the notion that the Minoans were pacifists. More likely, the whole island was united under the kings at Cnossus and the Minoan fleet provided sufficient protection against enemies from without.

The Minoans owed their success to their isolation and their ships. Isolation gave Crete a feeling of security, optimism, and lightheartedness reminiscent of early Egypt, but the lure of the sea resulted in a cultural dynamism that was distinctly un-Egyptian. Long before the Phoenicians ventured into the Mediterranean, Minoan seafarers were trading with Asia Minor, Syria, North Africa, the Aegean Islands, and even Spain. They imported tin and copper for the superb Minoan bronze ware that in turn became a chief item of export along with delicate polychrome pottery fashioned by Minoan artisans with consummate skill and taste. Minoan art is light and flowing; plants, animals, and marine life are portrayed with arresting naturalism. The artists produced no monumental works of sculpture but excelled at making small, exquisite statuettes. The Minoan style is characterized by grace rather than grandeur.

Minoan agriculture was devoted chiefly to the production of grain, wine, and olive oil—the so-called Mediterranean triad—which were also to be the chief agricultural commodities of classical Greece. The Minoan economy was exceptionally prosperous during the golden age of Crete. By about 1500 B.C. it had reached a level of complexity that required the keeping of extensive records on clay tablets, in a language as yet undeciphered that Sir Arthur Evans called Linear A.

Commercial prosperity enabled the Minoan aristocracy to live luxuriously. Women enjoyed a relatively high status in society. They are depicted in the statuettes and frescoes of the age dressed elaborately in hooped skirts with wasp waists, tight-fitting bodices that left the breasts exposed, and marvelously complex hairdos. A French archeologist was so charmed by a fresco of one of these elegant Minoan women that he named her *La Petite Parisienne*.

The lively spirit of the Minoans is nowhere better illustrated than in their love of games. Minoan art has left us scenes of

Minoan statuette, about 1700 B.C. [*Alison Frantz, Athens—Art Reference Bureau (Museum Heraklion)*].

boxing matches, acrobatics, and bull-leaping. The latter, which probably had a religious significance, involved both male and female athletes grasping a bull by the horns and leaping over its body. A group of curious scholars went to the length of asking an American cowboy how this might have been done, and were told flatly that it could not be done at all. Yet bull-leaping scenes abound in Minoan art, and we can only conclude that somehow it *was* done—perhaps through the joint efforts of superbly trained athletes and an unusually obliging bull.

Minoan religion has been a subject of much fascinating guesswork, but in the absence of decipherable religious texts we can be certain of nothing. A Minoan statuette of a stylishly dressed, bare-breasted young woman holding snakes might represent a fertility goddess, and might not. The absence of large temples in ancient Crete does suggest that the Minoans, like the later Greeks, put relatively little emphasis on priesthoods. Judging from the archeological evidence (which could well be misleading), the formal religious organization of Minoan society was much less conspicuous than that of most civilizations of the ancient Near East.

Hall of palace of Minos at Cnossus (*Marburg—Art Reference Bureau*).

THE MYCENAEAN GREEKS

Sometime around 2000 B.C. the first Greek-speaking peoples arrived in southern Greece. From about 1580 onward the Greek settlements were increasingly influenced by Minoan civilization, although they seem to have retained their political independence. Fortress cities such as Mycenae and Tiryns in the Peloponnesus dominated the surrounding country, and in time—if Homer's later testimony can be trusted—all the princes of southern Greece recognized the supremacy of the warrior kings of Mycenae.

The Mycenaean Greeks learned much from the Minoans; their culture differed from that of Crete chiefly in its emphasis on fortifications. They adapted the Minoan script (Linear A) to their

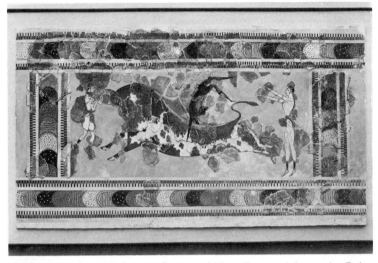

Bull-leaping; fresco Palace at Cnossus (*Alison Frantz, Athens —Art Reference Bureau*).

own different language. The result was Linear B, which used a Minoan syllabary to express Greek words. Their art, architecture, and customs were all strongly influenced by the Minoans; they even took up bull-leaping, and their women began adopting Minoan dress, hairdos, and cosmetics. (The painted face has traditionally been a mark of primitivism in men; of sophistication in women.)

Before long Mycenaean sailors were challenging the Cretan supremacy in the Aegean. In about 1475 a band of Greeks seems to have come to power in Cnossus itself, for thereafter the Cnossan records were kept in the Greek Linear B (which is found nowhere else on Crete). In about 1400 Minoan civilization was shaken severely when a devastating invasion of the island, probably by other Mycenaean Greeks, left the towns, villas, and palaces in ruins. The great palaces were never rebuilt on their previous scale, although there is evidence that Cnossus was inhabited for several generations thereafter.

With the disintegration of the Minoan state, Mycenaean ships became increasingly active in the trade of the eastern Mediterranean. Between about 1400 and 1200 the Mycenaeans grew rich on their commerce and flourished exceedingly. It is at the end of this period, perhaps around 1200, that King Agamemnon of Mycenae led the Greeks against Troy. But even at the time of the Trojan War the political stability of Mycenaean Greece was being disturbed by the emergence of the Dorian Greeks and related tribes. Traditionally, scholars have assumed that the Dorians invaded from the north, but recent investigations suggest that they may already have been settled in Greece as a subject people before their rise to power. Whatever the case, the Dorian Greeks were little affected by Minoan-Mycenaean culture, and they demolished it through military violence. Linear B tablets found in Mycenaean cities of about 1120 B.C. record frantic but vain preparations for defense. One after another, the Mycenaean cities were sacked and burned, and the civilization that had begun in Crete and later spread to the Greek mainland faded into legend.

THE GREEK DARK AGE: c. 1120 −800 B.C.

The destruction of Mycenaean culture was roughly concurrent with the collapse of the Hittites and the decline of the Egyptian New Kingdom. The far-flung maritime activities of the Phoenicians in the following epoch were made possible not only by the troubles of the Near Eastern empires but also by the disruption of Mycenaean commerce.

Between Mycenaean and classical Greece lies a chasm of several centuries known as the "dark age" of Hellenic history.* The Greeks lapsed into illiteracy, and when they began to write once again they did so not in the old Minoan syllabary but in an alphabet adapted from the Phoenicians. In the meantime, most of the Peloponnesus had fallen under the controls of the new Dorian Greeks, and the leadership of that area, once exercised by Mycenae, passed to the Dorian city of Sparta. Athens, as yet an unimportant town, became a haven for Mycenaean refugees. A group of Mycenaean Greeks known as Ionians fled across the

---

*Hellenic = Greek; Hellas = Greece.

Aegean and settled along the western coast of Asia Minor and on the islands offshore. Thenceforth, that region was known as Ionia and became an integral part of Greek civilization.*

In the chaotic conditions of dark-age Greece, political authority crumbled. The Greeks were divided into tribes which, in turn, were subdivided into clans. Each clan included a number of related families that had their own distinctive cult and held their lands and wealth in common. The sovereign powers once exercised by cities descended to the level of the elders of the tribes and clans.

HOMER

With the appearance of the Homeric epics in eighth century Ionia, the darkness began to lift. Both the *Iliad* and the *Odyssey* are the products of a long oral tradition carried on by the minstrels of Mycenaean and post-Mycenaean times who recited their songs of heroic deeds at the banquets of the nobility. Whether the epics in their final form were the work of one man or several is in dispute. A number of scholars doubt that the *Iliad* and the *Odyssey* could have had a common author. Someone has suggested facetiously that the epics should not be associated with Homer at all but with an entirely different person of the same name.

Both epics are filled with vivid accounts of battle and adventure, but at heart both are concerned with ultimate problems of human life. The *Iliad*, for example, depicts the tragic consequences of the quarrel between two sensitive, hot-tempered Greek leaders, Agamemnon and Achilles, toward the end of the Trojan War:

> Divine Muse, sing of the ruinous wrath of Achilles, Peleus' son, which brought ten thousand sorrows to the Greeks, sent the souls of many brave heroes down to the world of the dead, and left their bodies to be eaten by dogs and birds: and the will of Zeus was

*See the map on p. 81.

> fulfilled. Begin where they first quarreled, Agamem-
> non the King of Men, and great Achilles.*

Despite Homer's allusion to the will of Zeus, his characters are by no means puppets of the gods, even though divine intervention occurs repeatedly in his narrative. Rather they are intensely—sometimes violently—human, and they are doomed to suffer the consequences of their own deeds. In this respect, as in many others, Homer foreshadows the Greek tragic dramatists of the fifth century B.C.

Achilles' dazzling career with its harvest of ten thousand sorrows prefigures the career of Greece itself. The gods were said to have offered Achilles the alternatives of a long but humdrum life or glory and an early death. His choice symbolizes the meteoric course of Hellenic history.

Homer was the first literate European poet and he has never been surpassed. The *Iliad* and the *Odyssey* were the Old and New Testament of ancient Greece, studied by every Greek schoolchild and cherished by Greek writers and artists as an inexhaustible source of inspiration. The epics were typically Greek in their rigorous and economical organization around a single theme, their lucidity, their moments of tenderness that never slip into sentimentality—in short, their brilliantly successful synthesis of heart and mind.

THE HOMERIC GODS

The gods of Mt. Olympus, who play such a significant role in the Homeric poems, had diverse origins. Poseidon, the sea god, was Minoan; Zeus, the hurler of thunderbolts and ruler of Olympus, was a Dorian god; Aphrodite, the goddess of love, was an astral deity from Babylonia; Apollo and a number of others were local deities long before they entered the divine assemblage of Olympus. By Homer's time these diverse gods had been arranged into a hierarchy of related deities common to all Greeks. The Olympic gods were anthropomorphic; that is,

---

*Translated by H.D.F. Kitto in *The Greeks* (rev. ed., Penguin, 1957), p. 45.

they were human in form and personality, capable of rage, lust, jealousy, and all the other traits of the warrior-hero. But they also possessed immortality and other superhuman attributes. The universality of the Olympic cult served as an important unifying force that compensated in part for the localism that always characterized Greek politics. Yet each clan and each district also honored its own special gods, many of whom, like Athena the patron goddess of Athens, were represented in the Olympic pantheon. The worship of these local gods was associated with feelings of family devotion or regional and civic pride. The gods were concerned chiefly with the well-being of social groups rather than the prosperity or salvation of the individual, and their worship was almost indistinguishable from patriotism.

Ancient fertility deities rivaled the Olympians in popularity. Demeter, the goddess of grain, and Dionysus, the god of wine, were almost ignored in the Homeric epics but seem to have been at least as important to most Greeks as were the proud deities of Olympus. Eleusis, a small town near Athens, became the chief center for the worship of Demeter (whose name means "Earth Mother"), and the annual rites celebrated there, the Eleusinian Mysteries, dramatized the ancient myth of death and resurrection. For the Athenians, they were the most solemn of all religious observances: the yearly return of life-giving crops depended on the favor of Demeter.

The Greeks honored Dionysus, the god of wine, with wild orgies during which female worshipers would dance and scream through the night—though in time these rites became more sedate. Both Demeter and Dionysus offered their followers the hope of personal salvation and immortality that was absent from the Olympic religion.

Finally, and particularly among the lower social orders, animism persisted in all its numberless and exotic forms. The world of the Greek peasants, like that of their Near Eastern contemporaries, was literally crawling with gods.

Chapter
6

The Rise of Classical Greece

THE POLIS

By Homer's time, Greek culture was developing throughout the area around the Aegean Sea—in Ionia along the coast of Asia Minor, on the Aegean islands, in Athens and its surrounding district of Attica, in the Peloponnesus, and in other regions of mainland Greece.* But the Greek peoples did not coalesce into a single pan-Hellenic state. Political unity was discouraged by the roughness of the Ionian Coast, the obvious insularity of the islands, and the mountains and inlets that divided the Greek peninsula itself into a number of semi-isolated districts. The

---

*See the map on p. 100.

existence of the myriad city-states of ancient Greece cannot, however, be explained entirely by the environment. There are numerous examples of small independent states separated by no geographical barriers whatever—of several autonomous districts, for example, on a single island. Perhaps the Greeks lived in city-states simply as a matter of choice. Whatever the reason, classical Greek culture without the independent city-state is inconceivable.

We have used the term city-state to describe what the Greeks knew as the polis. Actually, polis is untranslatable, and city-state fails to convey its full meaning. In classical times the word was packed with emotional and intellectual content. Each polis had its own distinctive customs and its own gods and was an object of intense religious-patriotic devotion. More than a mere region, it was a community of citizens—the inhabitants of both town and surrounding district who enjoyed political rights and played a role in government. Words such as political, politics, and polity come from the Greek polis; to the Greeks, politics without the polis would be a contradiction in terms. Aristotle is often quoted as saying, "Man is a political animal"; what he really said was that man was a creature who belonged in a polis. In a vast empire like that of Persia, so the Greeks believed, slaves could live—barbarians could live—but not free and civilized people.

The polis was the Greeks' answer to the perennial conflict between the individual and the state, and perhaps no other human institution has succeeded in reconciling these two concepts so satisfactorily. The Greeks expressed their intense individualism *through* the polis, not in spite of it. The polis was sufficiently small that its members could behave and relate as individuals; the chief political virtue was participation, not obedience. Accordingly, the polis became the vessel of Greek creativity and the matrix of the Greek spirit. A unified pan-Hellenic state might have eliminated the intercity warfare that afflicted classical Greece. It might have brought peace, stability, and power, but at the sacrifice of the very institution that made classical Greece distinctive in human history.

Still, the system of independent warring poleis* was a re-

---

*"Poleis" is the plural of "polis."

markably inefficient basis for Greek political organization. The poleis were able to evolve and flourish only because they developed in a political vacuum. The Minoans were only a memory, and Macedonian and Roman imperialism lay in the future. During the formative period of the polis system in the ninth, eighth, and seventh centuries, the Assyrians were concerned primarily with maintaining their land empire and the seafaring Phoenicians were not a dangerous military power. The chief threat to the Greeks of the dark age was the violence of their own people. As a matter of security the inhabitants of a small district would often erect a citadel on some central hill that they called an acropolis (high town). The acropolis was the natural assembly place of the district in time of war and its chief religious center. As local commerce developed, an agora or market place usually arose at the foot of the acropolis, and many of the farmers whose fields were nearby built houses around the market, for reasons of sociability and defense.

THE SOCIAL ORDERS

At about the time that the polis was emerging, descendants of original tribal elders were evolving into a hereditary aristocracy. An occasional polis might be ruled by a king (*basileus*), but, generally speaking, monarchy was diminishing; often it was reduced to a ceremonial office. By about 700 B.C. or shortly thereafter, most Greek kings had been overthrown or shorn of all but their religious functions, leaving the aristocracy in full control. The aristocrats had meanwhile appropriated to themselves the lion's share of the lands that clan members had formerly held in common. Slowly the polis was replacing the clan as the object of primary allegiance and the focus of political activity, but the aristocracy rode out the waves of change, growing in wealth and power.

Below the aristocracy was a class of farmers who had managed to acquire fragments of the old clan common lands or who had developed new farms on virgin soil. They had no genuine voice in public affairs and their economic condition was always precarious. The Greek soil is the most barren in Europe, and while the large-scale cultivation of vine and olive usually brought prosperity and power to the aristocrats, the small farmers tended to sink from free status into dependency. Their condition was portrayed vividly by the eighth-century poet Hesiod, a farmer himself. In his *Works and Days* Hesiod described a world that had declined from a primitive golden age to the present "age of iron," characterized by a corrupt nobility. For the common farmer, life was "bad in winter, cruel in summer—never good." Yet Hesiod insists that righteousness will triumph in the end. In the meantime the farmer must work all the harder: "In the sweat of your face shall you eat bread." Out of an age in which the farmer's lot was declining, Hesiod proclaimed his faith in the ultimate victory of justice and the dignity of toil.

COLONIZATION: c. 750−550 B.C.

Even as Hesiod was writing his *Works and Days,* a movement was beginning that would bring a degree of relief to the small farmer and the still lower classes of the landless and dispossessed. By 750 B.C. the Greeks had once again taken to the sea—as pirates in search of booty or as merchants in search of copper and iron (rare in Greece) and the profits of trade. In this adventurous age a single Greek crew might raid and plunder one port and sell the loot as peaceful merchants in the next. During the course of their voyaging, the Greeks found many fertile districts ripe for colonization, and during the two centuries between about 750 and 550 B.C. a vast movement of colonial expansion occurred that was to transform not only Greece itself but the whole Mediterranean world.

A number of Greek poleis, great and small, now sent bands of colonists across the seas to found new communities on distant shores. In time some of these colonies sent out colonists of their own to establish still more settlements. The typical colonial polis, although bound to its mother city by ties of kinship, sentiment, and commerce, and a common patriotic cult, was politically independent. We cannot speak of colonial empires in this period; even the word "colony" is a little misleading.

The motives behind the colonial movement are to be found in the economic and social troubles afflicting the Greek homeland. Colonization meant new opportunities for those with little land

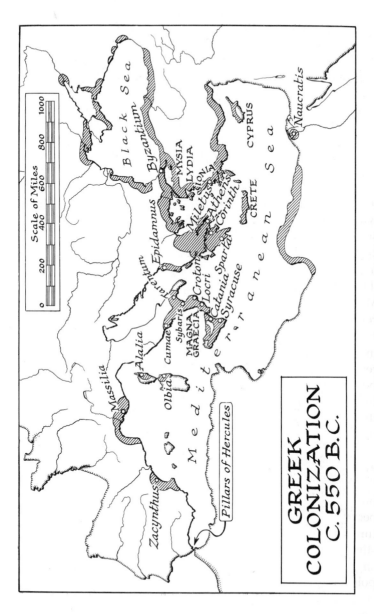

Greek colonization, 550 B.C.

and those with none. It provided the aristocracy with a useful safety valve against the pressures of rising population and accumulating discontent. And there were always a few adventurous or disaffected aristocrats to lead the enterprise. In the stark environment of the pioneer colony hard work was more likely to bring its reward than in the Greece of Hesiod. Here were all the opportunities for rapid social and economic advancement commonly associated with a frontier society.

In the course of two centuries or so, the Greek polis spread from the Aegean region far and wide along the coasts of the Mediterranean and the Black Sea. The Ionian polis of Miletus alone founded some eighty colonies. So many Greek settlements were established in southern Italy and Sicily that the whole area became known as *Magna Graecia*—Great Greece. The small colonial polis of Byzantium, dominating the trade route between the Black Sea and the Mediterranean, became, a millennium later, the capital of the East Roman Empire (under the name of Constantinople) and remained throughout the Middle Ages one of the greatest cities in the world. The Greek colony of Neopolis (New Polis) in southern Italy became the modern Napoli or Naples; Nikaia on the Riviera became the modern Nice; Massilia became Marseilles; Syracuse in Sicily remains to this day one of the island's chief cities. Through the poleis of *Magna Graecia* Greek culture was transmitted to the Romans, but this was merely one important episode in a process that saw the diffusion of Greek civilization all along the shores of southern Europe, North Africa, and western Asia.

The colonial experience was profoundly significant in the evolution of the Greek way of life. The flourishing commerce that developed between the far-flung Hellenic settlements brought renewed prosperity to Greece itself. The homeland became an important source of wine, olive oil, and manufactured goods for the colonies. The needs of the new settlements stimulated the growth of industrial and commercial classes: smiths and potters, stevedores and sailors, transformed many poleis from quiet agrarian communities into bustling mercantile centers. Coinage was introduced, on the Lydian model, and a new elite of merchants and manufacturers eased their way into the councils of government alongside the old noble families.

THE TYRANTS

The century from about 650 to 550 was an age of fundamental economic and political change. The introduction of coinage from Lydia was a boon to the mercantile elite but tended to amplify differences in wealth. It was in this age that the Ionian poet Pythermus wrote the golden line that alone of all his works has survived: "There's nothing else that matters—only money." The ever-increasing abundance of metal enabled the middle class to purchase the heavy armor necessary in the warfare of the day. And as a result, the mounted aristocratic army of earlier times began to give way in the early seventh century to a citizens' army of well-drilled, mailed foot soldiers called hoplites. Before long, the classes who fought for the polis began to demand a voice in its affairs.

Meanwhile, the colonial movement was waning. The best colonial sites were gradually occupied, and the rise of new powers like Carthage in the west and Lydia and Persia in the east prevented further expansion. As the safety valve slowly closed, the old pressures of economic and social discontent reasserted themselves. One after another the poleis of Greece and Ionia were torn by civil strife as the middle and lower classes rose against the wealthy and privileged. In many instances these conflicts resulted in the overthrow of aristocratic control by "tyrants" who, like many of their modern counterparts, claimed to govern in the interests of the common people.

To the Greeks a tyrant was not necessarily an evil ruler but simply one who rose to power without hereditary or legal claim. Typically, the tyrants did not smash the machinery of government but merely controlled it. They were upstarts, attuned to the currents of their age, who used the new coined money to hire armies of mercenaries and manipulated social discontent to their own advantage. Since they owed their power to the masses they sought to retain mass support by canceling or scaling down debts, sponsoring impressive public works projects, redistributing the lands of aristocrats, and reforming taxation. But in most Greek communities tyranny proved ephemeral. Some tyrants were overthrown by the older privileged classes; others by the middle and lower classes who, as they became increasingly

self-confident, sought to assume direct control of political affairs. By the opening of the fifth century the Greek political
structure displayed every imaginable configuration of upper,
lower, and middle class rule.

SPARTA

Sparta and Athens, the two dominant poleis of the fifth century,
stood at opposite ends of the Greek political spectrum. Neither
played an important role in the colonization movement, for both
adopted the alternative course of territorial expansion in their
own districts. But while Athens evolved through the traditional
stages of monarchy, aristocracy, tyranny, and democracy,
Sparta acquired a peculiar mixed political system that discouraged commerce, cultural inventiveness, and the amenities of life
for the sake of iron discipline and military efficiency.

During the eighth and seventh centuries Sparta underwent
the same political and social processes as other Greek states and
played a vigorous role in the development of Greek culture. Yet
from the beginning the Spartan spirit was singularly sober, and
military concerns were central to Spartan life. The severity of its
art and its Dorian architecture contrasted sharply with the
charming elegance of Ionia and the cultural dynamism of Attica.
Politically, Sparta had always been conservative. When the
aristocracy rose to power, the monarchy was not abolished but
merely weakened. With the rise of the commoners certain
democratic features were incorporated into the Spartan constitution yet the monarchy and aristocracy endured. Sparta could
adapt cautiously to new conditions but found it difficult to
abandon anything from its past.

Toward the end of the eighth century, when other Greek
states were beginning to relieve their social unrest and land
hunger by colonization, Sparta conquered the fertile neighboring district of Messenia, appropriating large portions of the
conquered land for its own citizens and reducing many Messenians to slavery. These unfortunate people, described by a
Spartan poet as "asses worn by loads intolerable," were Greeks
themselves and were much too proud to accept their enslavement with resignation. In the late seventh century the Spartans

crushed a Messenian revolt only after a desperate struggle. It now became clear that the Messenians could be held down only by strong military force and constant watchfulness. It was apparently at this point that Sparta transformed itself into a garrison state whose citizens became a standing army. Culture declined to the level of the barracks; the good life became the life of basic training.

Sparta became a tense, humorless society dedicated to the perpetuation, by force, of the status quo. Fear of Messenian rebellion grew into a collective paranoia as some 8000 Spartan citizens assumed the task of keeping many tens of thousands of restless slaves in a state of permanent repression. Between the citizens and the slaves was a group of free noncitizens, excluded from political life, who engaged in commercial activities forbidden to the citizens themselves. The state slaves of Sparta—the helots—included not only Messenians but other Greek families as well, some of whom had been enslaved during the original Dorian conquests. The Spartan state divided its lands into numerous lots, one for each citizen, and the helots who worked these lots relieved the citizens of all economic responsibility, freeing them for a life of military training and service to the state.

THE CONSTITUTION OF "LYCURGUS"

The writers of antiquity ascribed the Spartan constitution to a legendary lawgiver named Lycurgus. And although it drew from earlier Spartan traditions, the constitution operated with such rigorous logical consistency as to suggest the hand of a single author. Sparta had two kings whose powers had been greatly reduced by the sixth century. One or the other of them served as supreme commander on every military campaign, but at home their authority was overshadowed by that of three political bodies: (1) an aristocratic council of elders, (2) an executive board of five *ephors* elected from the whole citizenry, and (3) an assembly of citizens that included every Spartan male over thirty. Thus, Sparta was technically a democracy, although a limited one. Every citizen participated in the assembly, but citizenship was denied to many freemen, to all women, and (of course) to all slaves. The Spartan assembly had the function of approving or disapproving important questions of state, but it did so by acclamation rather than ballot and its members were not permitted to debate the issues. Accordingly, the assembly was by no means an area of rough and tumble political conflict. It was characterized instead by the same dreary conformity that overhung all Spartan life.

The lives of Sparta's citizens were tended and guided by the state from cradle to grave, always for the purpose of producing strong, courageous, highly disciplined soldiers. The introduction of styles, luxuries, and ideas from without was rigorously controlled. At a time when coinage was stimulating economic life elsewhere, Sparta used simple iron bars as its medium of exchange. Spartan citizens seldom left their homeland except on campaigns, and outsiders were discouraged from visiting Sparta. Infants were abandoned to die of exposure if they were puny or malformed. At the age of seven the Spartan boy was turned over to the state and spent his next thirteen years in a program of education in military skills, physical training, the endurance of hardships, and unquestioning devotion to the polis. The typical product of this system was patriotic, strong, and courageous, but incurious. At twenty he entered the citizen army and lived his next ten years in a barracks. He might marry, but he could visit his wife only if he was sufficiently resourceful to elude the barracks guards (this seems to have been regarded as a test of skill). At thirty he became a full-fledged citizen. He could now live at home, but he ate his meals at a public mess to which he was obliged to contribute the products of his assigned fields. The fare at these public messes was Spartan in the extreme. One visitor, after eating a typical meal, remarked, "Now I understand why the Spartans do not fear death."

The Spartan citizen had almost no individual existence; body and soul, he was dedicated to the state. If the helot's life was hard, so was the citizen's. Life in Sparta would seem to be a violent negation of Greek individualism, yet many Greeks were unashamed admirers of the Spartan regime. To them, Sparta represented the ultimate in self-denial and commitment to a logical idea. The Greeks admired the ordered life, and nowhere was life more ordered than in Sparta. To the Greek, there was a crucial difference between the helot and the Spartan citizen:

helots endured hardships because they had to, citizens because they *chose* to. And the Spartans always remembered that the object of their regime was the maintenance of the status quo— not aggressive imperialism. They were the best warriors in Greece, yet they employed their military advantage with restraint. To the accusation of artistic sterility a Spartan might reply that Sparta, with all its institutions directed toward a single ideal, was itself a work of art.

ATHENS

Athens dates from the Mycenaean Age, but not until much later did it become prominent in Greek politics and culture. By about 700 B.C. the earlier monarchy had been deprived of political power by the aristocracy, and the entire district of Attica had been united into a single state whose political and commercial center was Athens itself. But the free inhabitants of Attica became Athenian citizens, not Athenian slaves, and the district was held together by bonds of mutual allegiance rather than military might. To be an Attican was to be an Athenian.

The unification of Attica meant that the polis of Athens comprised a singularly extensive area, and consequently the Athenians suffered less severely from land hunger than many of their neighbors. Athens therefore sent out no colonists, yet as a town only four miles from the coast it was influenced by the revival of Greek commerce. Very slowly, new mercantile classes were developing. Athenian institutions were gradually modified, first to extend participation in public affairs to the lesser landed gentry, next to the merchants and manufacturers, and finally to the common citizens.

SOLON AND PISISTRATUS

In the 590s an aristocratic poet-statesman named Solon was given extraordinary powers to reform the laws of Athens. His reforms left the preponderance of political power in the hands of the wealthy but nevertheless moved significantly in the direction of democracy. Solon's laws abolished enslavement for default of debts and freed all debtors who had previously been enslaved. More important, the lowest classes of free Athenian males were now admitted into the popular assembly (whose powers were yet distinctly limited), and a system of popular courts was established whose judges were chosen by lot from among the entire citizenry without regard to wealth. For the Athenian, selection by lot was simply a means of putting the choice into the hands of the gods. Its consequence was to raise to important offices men who were their own masters and owed nothing to wealthy and influential political backers. Of course the system also produced a predictable quota of asses and nincompoops, but recent history attests that the elective principle is by no means immune to that fault. On the whole, selection by lot worked well in Athens and gradually became a characteristic feature of Athenian democracy.

Solon's laws were seen by many among the privileged classes as dangerously radical, but the lower classes demanded still more reforms. The consequence of this continued popular unrest was the rise of tyranny in Athens. Between 561 and 527 a colorful tyrant named Pisistratus dominated the Athenian government. Twice he was expelled by angry aristocrats; twice he returned with the support of the commoners. At length he achieved the elusive goal of all despots: he died in power and in bed.

Pisistratus was the best of all possible tyrants: he sponsored a lavish building program, patronized the arts, and revolutionized agriculture by confiscating estates of nobles and redistributing them among the small farmers. He established Athenian commercial outposts on the waterway linking the Aegean and Black Seas, thereby taking the first crucial steps along the road to empire. He gave Athens peace, prosperity, and a degree of social and economic harmony that it had long needed. The agrarian dilemma that had afflicted Attica for generations was effectively solved. Apart from some grumbling aristocrats, the polis was at peace with itself at last.

THE CONSTITUTION OF CLEISTHENES

Pisistratus' two sons and successors proved incompetent and oppressive. One was assassinated; the other was driven from power by exiled nobles who returned with Spartan military support. But many aristocrats had grown wise in exile and were willing to accept diminished estates and popular rule. Under the leadership of a statesmanlike aristocrat named Cleisthenes, a new and thoroughly democratic constitution was established in the closing decade of the sixth century which became the political basis of Athens' golden age. Cleisthenes administered a major blow to the aristocratic leaders of the old tribes and clans. Until the time of his reforms loyalty to clan and tribe had remained strong. Now Cleisthenes abolished their military and political functions, preserving only their ceremonial roles. For the purpose of systematic military recruitment, he established ten new "tribes" whose membership was no longer based on kinship. Each of the ten tribes was made up of numerous small territorial districts scattered throughout Attica. Consequently, members of every class—commercial, industrial, rural, and aristocratic—were about evenly divided among the ten tribes.

Cleisthenes may also have been responsible for introducing the principle of ostracism, which provided a further safeguard against violent factionalism.* Each year the Athenians decided by vote whether or not they would ostracize one of their number. If they decided affirmatively, then any citizen might propose the name of a person whom he considered a threat to the well-being of the polis. Whichever candidate received the most votes in the Assembly was banished from Athens for ten years. He kept his citizenship and his property but was no longer in a position to interfere with the operation of the polis.

All matters of public policy were decided by the Assembly, whose membership included all Athenian citizens from landless laborers to aristocrats. As in Sparta and elsewhere in Greece, citizenship was limited to males, but in Athens it came to include every freeman of eighteen years or over. The total citizenry of mid-fifth-century Athens has been estimated at about 50,000 men. There were also, exclusive of women and children, about 25,000 resident aliens called *metics* who were free but without political rights, and perhaps some 55,000 adults male slaves. When we speak of Athenian democracy we must always remember that a considerable group of Athenians were

---

*Ostracism may have been introduced into Athens at a somewhat later date. The first recorded use is in 488.

enslaved and that slaves and women had no voice in politics whatever. Nevertheless, citizenship was far less exclusive than in Sparta, and with respect to the citizenry itself Athens was more thoroughly democratic than any modern state. The citizens did not elect the legislators; they *were* the legislators.

For the transaction of day-to-day business, Cleisthenes provided a smaller body—a Council of Five Hundred—for which every Athenian citizen over thirty was eligible. The Council was made up of fifty men from each tribe chosen annually by lot from a list of tribal nominees. Each of these fifty-man tribal groups served for one-tenth of a year. Their order of rotation was determined by a crude machine which archeologists have recently discovered. It worked much like our modern bubble gum machines: a stone for each of the ten tribes was put in the machine, and each month one stone was released, thus preventing any tribe except the last from knowing in advance when its term would begin. Random selection pervaded the Athenian constitution. Every day a different chairman for the fifty-man panel was chosen by lot. Most of the various magistrates and civil servants also came to be selected by lot for limited terms and were strictly responsible to the Council of Five Hundred and the Assembly. This was a citizen's government in every sense of the word—a government of amateurs rather than professional bureaucrats.

Neither Council nor Assembly could provide the long-range personal leadership so essential to the well-being of the state. The Assembly was too unwieldy, the Council too circumscribed by rotation and lot. Consequently, direction of Athenian affairs came to be exercised by private citizens who had acquired great prestige and influence but did not necessarily occupy any official position. Such a person was known as a *prostates* of the *demos*—"leader of the people"—and his influence lasted only as long as his popularity.

Pericles, the great leader of fifth-century Athens, was precisely such a person, and his extended tenure in office illustrates the remarkable equilibrium achieved in the golden age between aristocratic leadership and popular sovereignty. Even Pericles was subject to the Assembly on which he depended for support. He could exercise his authority only by persuasion or political manipulation—never by force.

The success of the Greek polis in achieving harmony between the individual and society was nowhere more complete than in Athens, the scene of man's first significant encounter with democracy (though not woman's). The Athenian historian Thucydides celebrated this achievement in words he attributed to a speech by Pericles, intended to rouse Athenian spirits during the great war with Sparta:

> . . . Our constitution is called a democracy because it is in the hands not of the few but of the many. But our laws secure equal justice for all in their private disputes, not as a matter of privilege but as a reward of merit. . . . Alone of all states we regard a man who holds aloof from public life not as harmless but as useless; we deliberate in person all matters of policy, holding not that words and deeds go ill together, but that acts are foredoomed to failure when undertaken undiscussed. . . . In short, I say that Athens is the school of Hellas, and that her citizens yield to none, man for man, in independence of spirit, many-sidedness of attainment, and self-reliance in body and mind.*

---

*From Pericles' Funeral Oration, in Thucydides, *History of the Peloponnesian War.* I am following the translation of Sir Alfred Zimmern with slight modifications.

Chapter
7

The Zenith and Decline
of Classical Greece

IONIA, LYDIA, AND PERSIA

During the sixth century, while Solon, Pisistratus, and Cleisthenes were transforming Athens into a prosperous democracy,
the cultural center of the Hellenic world was Ionia. There, on the
shores of Asia Minor, the Greeks came into direct contact with
the culture of the ancient Near East. The results of this contact
were fruitful indeed, for the Ionian Greeks adapted Near
Eastern art, architecture, literature, and learning to their own
distinctive outlook. They created a brilliant, elegant culture,
more gracious and luxurious than any that existed in Greece
itself. It was in this setting that Greek philosophy, science, and
lyric poetry were born. Ionian poleis underwent much the same

political and economic developments as those of Greece, and by the sixth century the lower classes were attempting to diminish the control of aristocrats. In the Ionian city of Miletus, aristocrats and commoners went to the extreme of burning one another alive.

These internal social conflicts were affected drastically by the intervention of outside powers. During the 560s and 550s the coastal cities of Ionia fell one by one under the control of the Lydians, and when Cyrus the Great conquered Lydia in 546 they passed into the Persian Empire. In 499 the Ionian cities rebelled against Persia, and the Athenians were persuaded to send twenty ships to aid their desperate compatriots. But the Athenian aid proved insufficient and by 494 the Persians had crushed the insurrection, punctuating their victory by sacking Miletus. Ionia's gamble for independence had failed, and Darius the Great of Persia was now bent on revenge against Athens. The Persian Wars, Herodotus observed, were precipitated by the sending of twenty ships.

THE PERSIAN WARS: 490–479 B.C.

In 490 Darius led an army across the Aegean to teach the Greeks a lesson in respect. As was so often the case, the Greeks, even in the face of this calamity, found it impossible to unite. The Spartans held aloof in the Peloponnesus, claiming that they could not send their army until the moon's phase was auspicious, and other city-states preferred to await further developments. Consequently Athens was obliged to face the Persians almost alone. At Marathon in Attica the two armies met, and the Athenian hoplites, fighting shoulder to shoulder for the preservation of their homes and their polis, won a brilliant victory. 6400 Persians fell at Marathon while only 192 Greeks lost their lives.

Marathon was not won by Athenian heroism alone. Although outnumbered, the Athenians were better armed (the Persians were said to have used wicker shields), and the Persian army lacked its accustomed cavalry. Nevertheless, the Athenian victory was a notable achievement. It won Greece an invaluable postponement of the Persian threat, and it generated in Athens a powerful sense of pride and self-confidence. The sovereign of the world's greatest empire had been defeated by a small army of free Athenian citizens. For such men as these, so it seemed, nothing was impossible. The epitaph attributed to the great Athenian dramatist Aeschylus includes no mention of his literary achievements but only the proud statement that he had fought at Marathon.

The buoyant optimism that filled Athens in the wake of Marathon was tempered by the sobering thought that the Persians were likely to return in far greater numbers. Darius spent his last years planning a devastating new attack against Greece, but when the second invasion came, in 480, it was led by Darius' successor, Xerxes. A Persian army of about 180,000 fighting men, stupendous by the standards of the age, moved by land around the northern Aegean shore supported by a powerful armada.

Xerxes had paved his way into Greece by alliances with a number of opportunistic Greek cities such as Argos and Thebes. In the meantime Athens had been preparing for the onslaught under the enterprising leadership of Themistocles, a statesman of great strategic imagination who saw clearly that Athens' one hope was to build a strong fleet and seize control of the Aegean from the Persian Empire. By the time Xerxes led his forces into Greece, Themistocles' fleet was ready.

Sparta had by now awakened to the danger of a Persian conquest and was equally alarmed at the possibility of Athens winning additional prestige from another single-handed victory. During the sixth century Sparta had aimed its wars and diplomacy toward the establishment of a regional defensive alliance known as the Peloponnesian League. By the end of the century nearly every state in the Peloponnesus had joined the League, including the wealthy commercial polis of Corinth. Each League member had one vote, but Sparta alone had the privilege of summoning and presiding over the League's assembly and was usually able to dominate it. Now, in the shadow of Xerxes' invasion, representatives of the Peloponnesian states met at Corinth with delegates from Athens and a number of other poleis. Here they agreed to form a much larger organization—a Pan-Hellenic League—to coordinate the common defense.

As Xerxes moved southward through northern Greece, a small army of Spartans and other Greeks led by the Spartan King Leonidas placed itself across the Persian path at Thermopylae, a narrow pass between sea and mountains through which Xerxes' host had to move before breaking into the south. When the two armies met, the Persians found that their immense numerical superiority was of little use on so restricted a battlefield and that man for man they were no match for the Greeks. But at length a Greek turncoat led a contingent of the Persian army along a poorly defended path through the mountains to the rear of the Greek position. Now completely surrounded, the Greeks continued to fight—and died to the last man in defense of the field.

Although the battle of Thermopylae was a defeat for the Spartans, it became a long-remembered symbol of their dedication and courage. The inscription that was later placed over their graves is a model of Spartan brevity and understatement:

Tell them the news in Sparta, passer by,
*That here, obedient to their words, we lie.**

Much delayed, Xerxes' army now moved on Athens. The Athenians, at Themistocles' bidding, evacuated Attica and took refuge elsewhere, some in the Peloponnesus, others on the island of Salamis just off the Attic coast. The refugees on the island had to look on helplessly as the Persians plundered Athens and burned the temples on the Acropolis. But Themistocles' strategy was vindicated when the Greek and Persian fleets fought a decisive naval engagement in the Bay of Salamis. The Bay provided insufficient room for the huge Persian armada to maneuver, and the smaller but heavier Greek fleet, with the new Athenian navy as its core, pulled alongside the Persian ships and overwhelmed them with marines.

---

*Yet, paradoxically, the probable author of this epigram, Simonides, was not a Spartan. Poets do not abound in a barracks state.

Persia's navy was decimated before the eyes of Xerxes, who witnessed the disaster from a rocky headland. Commanding his army to withdraw to northern Greece for the winter, Xerxes himself departed for Asia never to return. In the following spring (479) the Persian army was routed at Plataea on the northern frontier of Attica by a Pan-Hellenic army under Spartan command. And the Greeks won a final victory over the tattered remnants of the Persian army and fleet at Cape Mycale in Ionia. Now, one after another, the Ionian cities broke loose from Persian control. Hellas had preserved its independence and was free to work out its own destiny.

As an ironic postscript, Themistocles fell from power shortly after his triumph at Salamis. Exiled from Athens, he ended his days in the service of the king of Persia.

THE ATHENIAN EMPIRE

To some historians the moment of truth for classical Greece was not Marathon, Salamis, or Plataea, but rather the brief period immediately afterward when the possibility of establishing the Pan-Hellenic League on a permanent basis was allowed to slip by. Yet it has always been easier to unite against a common foe than to maintain a wartime confederation in the absence of military necessity. Common fear is a stronger cement than common hope, and the creation of a Pan-Hellenic state from the Greek alliance of 480–479 B.C. was of the same order of difficulty as the creation of a World State from the United Nations of World War II. Considering the intense involvement of the typical Greek citizen in his polis, it seems doubtful that Greek federalism was ever a genuine option.

Nevertheless, the Greek world in 479, lacking our hindsight, could not be certain that the Persian invasions were truly over. Sparta, always fearful of a helot revolt at home, withdrew from the alliance, along with the other cities of the Peloponnesian League. Athens, however, was unwilling to lower its guard. A large fleet had to be kept in readiness, and such a fleet could not be maintained by Athens alone. Consequently, in 477 a new alliance was formed under Athenian leadership that included

most of the maritime poleis on the coasts and islands of the
Aegean from Attica to Ionia.

The alliance was known as the Delian League because its
headquarters and treasury were on the island of Delos, an
ancient religious center off the Ionian coast. Athens and a few
other cities contributed ships to the Delian fleet; the remaining
members contributed money. All were entitled to a voice in the
affairs of the Delian League, but Athens, with its superior
wealth and power, gradually assumed a dominant position.

Slowly the Delian League evolved into an Athenian Empire.
In 454 the League's treasury was transferred from Delos to
Athens, where its funds were diverted to the welfare and
adornment of Athens itself. The Athenians justified this financial sleight of hand with the argument that their fleet remained
always vigilant and ready to protect League members from
Persian aggression, but their explanation was received unsym-
pathetically in some quarters. A party of touring Ionians visiting
Athens might well admire the magnificent new temples being
erected on the Acropolis, but their admiration would be chilled
by the reflection that their own cities were contributing to the
building fund.

Some members tried to withdraw from the League, both
before and after the transfer of the treasury. But they quickly
discovered that Athens regarded secession as illegal and was
ready to enforce the continued membership of disillusioned
poleis by military action. With the development of this policy in
the 460s, and the relocation of the treasury in 454, the transformation from Delian League to Athenian Empire was complete.

The half century between Salamis and the opening of the
Peloponnesian War (480–431) was the Athenian golden age.
The empire rose and flourished, bringing Athens unimagined
wealth, not merely from imperial assessments but also from the
splendid commercial opportunities offered by Athenian domination of the Aegean. Athens was now the commercial hub of
the eastern Mediterranean world and the great power in Greece.
Sparta and her Peloponnesian allies held aloof, yet Athenian
statesmen such as Pericles hoped that one day they too would
be brought under Athens' sway.

THE GOLDEN AGE

The economic and imperialistic foundations of Athens' golden age are interesting to us chiefly as a backdrop for the cultural explosion that has echoed through the centuries of Mediterranean and European civilizations. Through a rare and elusive conjunction of circumstances, a group of some 50,000 politically conscious Athenian citizens created in the decades after Salamis a unique, many-sided culture of superb taste and unsurpassed excellence. The culture of the golden age was anticipated in the sixth and even earlier centuries, and the period of creativity continued into the fourth century and beyond. But the zenith of Greek culture was reached in imperial Athens during the time of Pericles, in the middle decades of the fifth century. The next two chapters will examine this cultural flowering more closely.

Despite its glittering achievements, the golden age of Athens was no means a utopia. The architecture and sculpture of the Acropolis, the tragic dramas, and the probing philosophical speculation were produced against a background of large-scale slavery, petty politics, and commercial greed. The status of Athenian women was as low or lower than at any other time in Greco-Roman antiquity. Whereas in Sparta and other Dorian cities of the time women could own property, in Athens they could not.

The age of Pericles was also marked by growing imperial arrogance. Pericles, whose popularity remained largely unchallenged from 461 to his death in 429, provided much-needed direction to democratic Athens, but he maintained the support of the commercial classes by advocating an ever-expanding empire.

Pericles' policy of extending Athenian dominion across the Greek world aroused the hostility of Sparta and its Peloponnesian League. Corinth, the second greatest power in the League and Athens' chief commercial rival, was especially alarmed at Pericles' imperialism. In 431 these accumulating tensions resulted in a war between the Peloponnesian League and the Athenian Empire—a protracted, agonizing struggle that ultimately destroyed the Athenian Empire and shook the Greek political structure to its foundations. The fifth century saw the polis system at its best and at its worst: on the one hand, the culture of Periclean Athens; on the other, the Peloponnesian War.

THE PELOPONNESIAN WAR

The war ran from 431 to 404 B.C. For the most part it was a matter of a whale fighting an elephant. Athens was invincible by sea, Sparta, by land. When the Spartans marched into Attica year after year to devastate the fields, the population would withdraw behind the protection of Athens' walls and live off foodstuffs imported by the fleet.

Democratic Athens and regimented Sparta represented two contrary political systems, and the disparity was intensified by the fact that each of the two tended to reproduce its own political structure in the states dependent on it. Sparta encouraged oligarchy (rule by the few) throughout the Peloponnesus while Athens was inclined to support democratic factions within the cities of its empire. Yet the Peloponnesian War was not so much an ideological conflict as a simple power struggle. Athens dreamed of bringing all Hellas under its sway, and Sparta and its allies were determined to end the threat of Athenian imperialism. Athens was coming to be regarded as a tyrant among the states of its own empire, but so long as Athenian ships patrolled the Aegean, rebellion was minimized. Paradoxically, the mother of democracies was driven to ever more despotic expedients to hold her empire together.

In 430 and 429 Athens, crowded with refugees, was struck by a plague that carried off perhaps a quarter of its population including Pericles himself. The loss of this far-sighted statesman, combined with the terrible shock of the plague, led to a rapid deterioration in the quality of Athenian government. Leadership passed into the hands of extremists, and the democracy acquired many of the worst characteristics of mob rule. A general who, through no fault of his own, failed to win some battle might be sent into exile. (Such was the experience of Thucydides, Athens' greatest historian). When the Athenians captured the island of Melos, an innocent neutral in the strug-

GREECE AT THE BEGINNING OF THE PELOPONNESIAN WAR, 431 B.C.

Athens and Allies
Sparta and Allies
Neutral
□ Capitals

Scale of Miles
0 20 40 60 80 100

Black Sea

Propontis

Hellespont

ANATOLIA

IONIA

LYCIA

Miletus

Mitylene

SAMOS

LESBOS

CHIOS

RHODES

NAXOS

Aegean Sea

MELOS

CRETE

CHALCIDICE

MACEDONIA

THESSALY

EUBOEA

Pydna

Pella

BOEOTIA

Thebes

□ Athens

Megara

Delphi

EPIRUS

ACHAEA

□ Corinth

PELOPONNESUS

Argos

MESSENIA

Sparta

LACONIA

Pylos

ACARNANIA

CORCYRA

Ionian Sea

gle, all its men were slaughtered and its women and children sold as slaves.

Pericles observed on the eve of the war that he was more afraid of Athens' mistakes than of Sparta's designs. His fear was well-founded, for as the war progressed along its dreary course Athenian strategy became increasingly reckless. The better part of the Athenian fleet was lost when two ill-planned expeditions against distant Syracuse ended in disaster. As Athens' grip on the Aegean loosened, its subject cities began to rebel, and at length a Peloponnesian fleet, financed in part by Persian gold, destroyed what was left of Athens' navy.

In 404 the Athenians surrendered—their wealth lost, their spirit broken, and their empire in ruins. Long thereafter Athens remained the intellectual and cultural center of the Greek world—it was even able to make something of an economic and political recovery—but its years of imperial supremacy were over.

THE FOURTH CENTURY

The period between the end of the Peloponnesian War in 404 and the Macedonian conquest of Greece in 338 was an age of chaos and anticlimax during which the polis system was drained and demoralized by intercity warfare. Athens' surrender left Sparta the dominant power in the Greek world, but only for a time. The victorious Spartan fleet had been built with Persian money, and Sparta paid her debt by allowing Persia to reoccupy Ionia. The Spartans were much too conservative to be successful imperialists, and although for a time they followed a policy of establishing oligarchic regimes in the poleis of Athens' former empire—indeed, in Athens itself—they quickly proved incapable of giving direction to Hellas.

In Athens and in many other states the oligarchies were soon overthrown, and Greece passed into a bewildering period of military strife and shifting hegemonies. For a brief period Thebes rose to supremacy. Athens began to form a new Aegean league only to be frustrated by Persian intervention. In the middle decades of the fourth century power tended to shift between Sparta, Athens, and Thebes, while the Greek colony of Syracuse dominated Sicily and southern Italy. Envoys from

Persia, always well supplied with money, saw to it that no one state became too powerful. A Greece divided and decimated by warfare could be no threat to the Persian Empire.

Ironically, Persia's diplomacy opened the way for an event that it had been determined at all costs to avoid: the unification of Greece. The debilitating intercity wars left Greece unprepared for the intervention of a new power on its northern frontier. Macedon (or Macedonia) was a kingdom whose inhabitants, although Greek, were centuries behind other Greeks in their political and cultural development—a warrior kingdom evoking the days of Homer's heroes. In 359 a talented opportunist named Philip became king of Macedon. He tamed and unified the Macedonian tribes, secured his northern frontiers, and then began a patient and artful campaign to bring all Greece under his control.

Having spent three years of his boyhood as a hostage in Thebes, Philip of Macedon had acquired a full appreciation of both Greek culture and Greek political instability. He hired the philosopher Aristotle as tutor for his son Alexander; he exploited the ever-increasing Greek distaste for war by fighting, bluffing, and cajoling his way into the south. He accompanied his conquests with repeated declarations of his peaceful intentions, and when at last Athens and Thebes resolved their ancient rivalry and joined forces against him it was much too late. At Chaeronea in 338, Philip won the decisive battle and Greece lay at his mercy.

Philip allowed the Greek states to run their own internal affairs but he organized them into a league whose policies he controlled. With the subordination of Greek independence to the will of King Philip, the classical age of Greek history came to an end. The accession of Philip's illustrious son, Alexander the Great, two years later, launched a new age that would spread Greek culture throughout the Near East and transform Greek life into something drastically different from what it had been before.

THE DECLINE OF THE POLIS

Classical Greece was a product of the polis, and when the polis lost its meaning classical Greece came to an end. The essence of the polis was participation in the political and cultural life of the community. The citizen was expected to take care of his private business and at the same time attend the assembly, participate in decisions of state, serve in the administration, and fight in the army or navy whenever necessary. Statesmen such as Pericles were at once administrators, orators, and generals. The polis at its best was a community of well-rounded citizens, with many interests and capabilities—in short, amateurs.

In the sixth and early fifth centuries, when Greek life had been comparatively simple, it was possible for one person to play many roles. But as the fifth century progressed the advantages of specialization grew. Military tactics became more complex. Administrative procedures became increasingly refined. Oratory became the subject of specialized study. As the various intellectual disciplines developed, it became more and more difficult to master them. The age of the amateur gave way to the age of the professional. The polis of the fourth century was filled with professional administrators, orators, scholars, bankers, sailors, and merchants, whose demanding careers left them time for little else. Citizens were becoming absorbed in their private affairs, and political life, once the very embodiment of the Greek spirit, was losing its fascination. Citizen-soldiers gave way increasingly to mercenaries, partly because civic patriotism was running dry but also because fighting was now a full-time career. The precarious equilibrium achieved in the golden age between competence and versatility—between individual and community—could only be momentary, for the intense creativity of the fifth century led inevitably to the specialization of the fourth. It has been said that "Progress broke the Polis,"* yet progress was a fundamental ingredient of the way of life that the polis created.

---

*Kitto, *The Greeks*, p. 161.

Chapter
8
The Hellenic Mind

The intellectual achievement of the Greeks has been of immense importance to Western Civilization. The civilizations of the ancient Near East did significant pioneer work in mathematics, engineering, and practical science; the Hebrews developed a profound ethical system based on the revelation of the one, all-powerful Creator-God. But it was the Greeks who first took the step of examining humanity and the cosmos from a rational standpoint. It was they who transcended the mythical and poetic approach to cosmology and began to look at the universe as a natural rather than a supernatural phenomenon, based on discoverable principles of cause and effect rather than on divine will. It was they who first attempted to base morality and the good life on reason.

Accordingly, the Greeks were the first philosophers—the first logicians—the first theoretical scientists. The Babylonians had studied the stars to prophesy; the Egyptians had mastered geometry to build tombs, and chemistry to create mummies. The Greeks had much to learn from their predecessors, but they turned their knowledge and their investigation toward a new end: a rational understanding of humanity and the universe. Their achievement has been described as "the discovery of the mind."

This is not to say that the Greeks were irreligious. Their dramas, their civic festivals, their Olympic Games were all religious celebrations; their art and architecture were devoted largely to honoring the gods; their generals sometimes altered strategy on the basis of some divine portent. But the Greek philosophers succeeded by and large in holding their gods at bay and untangling the natural from the supernatural. Like the Jews, they rejected the "I-thou" relationship of humanity and nature, but unlike the Jews they were not intensely involved in the worship of a single, omnipotent deity. The Greeks had no powerful official priesthood to enforce correct doctrine. To them, as to other ancient peoples, the cosmos was awesome. But they possessed the open-mindedness and audacity to probe it with their intellects.

IONIA: THE LYRIC POETS

Open-mindedness and audacity—so alien to the monarchies of the Near East—were nourished by the free and turbulent atmosphere of the polis. Greek rationalism was a product of Greek individualism, and among the first manifestations of this new spirit of self-awareness and irreverence for tradition was the development of lyric poetry in seventh- and sixth-century Ionia.

Greek lyric poetry was a literary achievement, but its importance transcends the field of belles lettres. The works of lyric poets such as Archilochus in the seventh century and Sappho of Lesbos in the sixth disclose a self-consciousness and intensity of experience far exceeding anything before. At a time when Spartan mothers were sending their sons to war with the stern admonition, "Return with your shield—or on it," the Ionian Archilochus was expressing a more individualistic viewpoint:

Some lucky Thracian has my shield,
  For, being somewhat flurried,
I dropped it by a wayside bush,
  As from the field I hurried;
Thank God, I made it clear away,
  To blazes with the shield!
I'll get another just as good
  When next I take the field.

With such lines as these Archilochus ceases to be a mere name and emerges as a vivid, engaging personality. He is history's first articulate coward.

The most intensely personal of the lyric poets was Sappho, an aristocratic woman of sixth-century Lesbos, who became the directress of a school for young girls—apparently a combination finishing school and religious guild dedicated to Aphrodite, the goddess of Love. Her passionate love lyrics to her students have raised puritanical eyebrows and have given enduring meaning to the word lesbian; the people of antiquity saw Sappho as the Tenth Muse and the equal of Homer. Never before had human feelings been expressed with such perception and sensitivity:

Love has unbound my limbs and set me shaking
A monster bitter-sweet and my unmaking.*

THE IONIAN PHILOSOPHERS

The same surge of individualism that produced lyric poetry gave rise to humanity's first effort to understand rationally the physical universe. So far as we know the first philosopher and theoretical scientist in human history was the sixth-century Ionian, Thales of Miletus, who set forth the proposition that water was the primal element of the universe. This hypothesis, although crude by present standards, constitutes a significant effort to impose a principle of intellectual unity on the diversity of experience. The world was to be understood as a single physical substance. Presumably solid objects were made of

---

*Greek Literature in Translation, ed. Oates and Murphy, p. 972.

compressed water, air of rarefied water, and empty space of dehydrated water. Thales' hypothesis did not commend itself to his successors, but the crucial point is that Thales had successors—that others, following his example, would continue the effort to explain the universe through natural rather than supernatural principles. Intellectual history had taken a bold new turn.

The Ionian philosophers after Thales continued to speculate about the primal substance of the universe. One suggested that air was the basic element; another, fire. The Ionian Anaximander set forth a primitive theory of evolution and declared that people were descended from fish. But these intellectual pioneers, their originality notwithstanding, disclose a basic weakness that characterized Greek thought throughout the classical age: an all-too-human tendency to rush into sweeping generalizations on the basis of a grossly inadequate factual foundation. Beguiled by the potentialities of rational inquiry, they failed to appreciate how painfully difficult it is to arrive at sound conclusions. Consequently, the hypotheses of the Ionians are of the nature of inspired guesses. Anaximander's theory of evolution, for example, was quickly forgotten because, unlike Darwin's, it had not significant supporting data.

THE PYTHAGOREAN SCHOOL

Pythagoras (c. 582–507 B.C.) represents a different intellectual trend. A native of Ionia, he migrated to southern Italy where he founded a brotherhood, half scientific, half mystical. He drew heavily from the mystery cults of Dionysus and Demeter. He was influenced especially by Orphism, a salvation cult that was becoming popular in the sixth century. The cult of Orpheus stressed guilt and atonement, a variety of ascetic practices, and an afterlife of suffering or bliss depending on the purity of one's soul. This and similar cults appealed to those who found inadequate solace in the heroic but worldly gods of Olympus.

Following the basic structure of Orphic dogma, Pythagoras and his followers advocated the doctrine of transmigration of souls and the concept of a quasi-monastic communal life. Enmeshed in all this was their profoundly significant notion that the basic element in nature was neither water, air, nor fire, but *number*. The Pythagoreans studied the intervals between musical tones and worked out basic laws of harmony. Having demonstrated the relationship between music and mathematics, they next applied these principles to the whole universe, asserting that the cosmos obeyed the laws of harmony and, indeed, that the planets in their courses produced musical tones which combined into a cosmic rhapsody: the music of the spheres. Implicit in this bewildering mixture of insight and fancy is the pregnant concept that nature is best understood mathematically.

Their mathematical thought was clouded by a superstitious reverence for the number ten which they saw as magical. Consequently, they have inspired a great deal of numerological foolishness down to our own day. But they also played a crucial role in the development of mathematics and mathematical science. They produced the Pythagorean theorem and the multiplication table, and their notions contributed to the development of modern science in the sixteenth and seventeenth centuries. The Greeks were at their best in mathematics, for here they could reason deductively—from self-evident concepts— and their distaste for the slow, patient accumulation of data was no hindrance.

THE FIFTH CENTURY

In the course of the fifth century, Greek thinkers raised and explored a great many of the central problems that have occupied philosophers ever since: whether the universe is in a state of flux or eternally changeless; whether it is composed of one substance or many; whether or not the nature of the universe can be grasped by the reasoning mind. Democritus (fl. 440) set forth a doctrine of materialism that anticipated several of the views of modern science. He maintained that the universe consists of countless atoms in random configurations—that it has no center and no periphery but is much the same one place as another. In short, the universe is infinite and the earth is in no way unique. Like Anaximander's theory of evolution, Democritus' atomism was essentially a philosophical assertion rather than a scientific hypothesis based on empirical evidence, and since infinity was not a concept congenial to the Greek mind, atomism long remained a minority view. But in early modern times Democritus' notion of an infinite universe contributed to the development of a new philosophical outlook and to the rise of modern astronomy.

It was in medicine and history rather than in cosmology that the Greeks of the fifth century were able to resist the lure of premature generalization and concentrate on the humble but essential task of accumulating accurate data. In the field of medicine, Hippocrates and his followers recorded case histories with scrupulous care and avoided the facile and hasty conclusion. Their painstaking clinical studies and their rejection of supernatural causation launched medicine on its modern career.

A similar reverence for the verifiable fact was demonstrated by the Greek historians of the period. History, in the modern sense, begins with Herodotus, a man of boundless curiosity who, in the course of his extensive travels, gathered a vast accumulation of data for his brilliant and entertaining history of the Persian Wars. Herodotus made a serious effort to separate fact from fable, but he was far surpassed in this regard by Thucydides, a disgraced Athenian general who wrote his account of the Peloponnesian War with unprecedented objectivity and an acute sense of historical criticism. "Of the events of the war," writes Thucydides, ". . . I have described nothing but what I either saw myself or learned from others whom I questioned most carefully and specifically. The task was laborious, because eyewitnesses of the same events gave different accounts of them, as they remembered or were interested in the actions of one side or the other."

Thucydides' philosophy of history differed radically from that of the Hebrews. To him, history was not a product of divine planning but rather the outgrowth of political action on the part of statesmen and popular assemblies. His approach was not social or economic as is that of many modern historians, but political and psychological. His chief interest lay in the motivations underlying political action, and he subjected the political conflicts in the Greek poleis to keen, rigorous analysis. To Thucydides, the polis was a fascinating arena of contending political views, and since he tended to see political issues as the

central problems of existence, he ascribed to the polis a dominant role in the dynamics of history. Here, as elsewhere,
Thucydides' thought was characteristically Greek.

THE SOPHISTS

In philosophy, history, and science, reason was winning its
victories at the expense of the supernatural. The anthropomorphic gods of Olympus were especially susceptible to rational
criticism, for few people acquainted with Ionian philosophy or
the new traditions of scientific history and medicine could
seriously believe that Zeus hurled thunderbolts or that Poseidon
caused earthquakes. Some came to see Zeus as a transcendent
god of the universe; others rejected him altogether.

But one who doubts that Zeus tosses thunderbolts might also
doubt that Athena protects Athens. And the rejection of Athena
and other civic deities was clearly subversive to the traditional
spirit of the polis. Religious skepticism was gradually undermin-
ing civic patriotism, and as skepticism advanced, patriotism
receded. Once again we are brought face to face with the
dynamic and paradoxical nature of the Greek experience: the
polis produced the inquiring mind, but in time the inquiring
mind eroded the most fundamental traditions of the polis.

The arch skeptics of fifth-century Athens were the Sophists, a
diverse group of professional teachers drawn from every corner
of the Greek world by the wealth of the imperial city. Much of
our information about the Sophists comes from the writings of
Plato, who disliked them heartily and portrayed them as intellectual prostitutes and tricksters. In reality most of them were
dedicated to the life of reason and the sound argument.

Unlike the Ionian philosophers, the fifth-century Sophists
were chiefly interested in human behavior rather than the
cosmos. They investigated ethics, politics, history, and psychol-
ogy and have been called the first social scientists. In applying
reason to these areas and teaching their students to do the same,
they aroused the wrath of conservatives and doubtless encouraged an irreverent attitude toward tradition. Of course the
Greeks were not nearly so tradition-bound as other peoples of
their era, but there is a limit to the amount of skepticism and

change that any social system can absorb. Many of the Sophists taught their pupils techniques of debating and getting ahead, while questioning the traditional doctrines of religion, patriotism, and dedication to the welfare of the community. Plato describes one of them as advocating the maxim that might makes right. Collectively, the Sophists stimulated an attitude of doubt, relativism, and ambitious individualism, thereby contributing to the dissolution of the polis spirit.

SOCRATES (469–399)

Socrates, the patron saint of intellectuals, was at once a part of this movement and an opponent of it. During the troubled years of the Peloponnesian War he wandered the streets of Athens teaching his followers to test their beliefs and preconceptions with the tool of reason. "An uncriticized life," he observed, "is scarcely worth living."

Like the Sophists, Socrates was interested in human rather than cosmic matters, but unlike many of them he was dissatisfied merely with tearing down traditional beliefs. He cleared the ground by posing seemingly innocent questions to his listeners that invariably entangled them in a hopeless maze of contradictions; but having devastated their opinions he substituted closely reasoned conclusions of his own on the subject of ethics and the good life. Knowledge, he taught, was synonymous with virtue, for a person who knew the truth would act righteously. Impelled by this optimistic conviction, he continued to attack cherished beliefs—to play the role of "gadfly" as he put it.

Gadflies have seldom been popular. The Athenians, put on edge by their defeat at Sparta's hands (which was hastened by the treachery of one of Socrates' pupils), could at last bear him no longer. In 399 he was brought to trial for denying the gods and corrupting youth and was condemned by a close vote. In accordance with Athenian law, he was given the opportunity to propose his own punishment. He suggested that the Athenians punish him by giving him free meals at public expense for the rest of his life. By refusing to take the business seriously, he was in effect condemning himself to death. Declining an opportunity to escape into exile, he was executed by poison. He expired with the cheerful observation that at last he had the opportunity of discovering for himself the truth about the afterlife.

PLATO (427–347)

Socrates would not have made good on an American university faculty, for although he was a splendid teacher, he did not publish.* We know of his teachings largely through the works of his student Plato, one of history's towering intellects and a prolific and graceful writer.

In his *Republic*, Plato outlined the perfect polis—the first utopia in literary history. Here, ironically, the philosopher rejected the democracy that he knew and described an ideal state more Spartan than Athenian. Farmers, workers, and merchants were without political rights; a warrior class, trained with Spartan rigor, defended the state, and an intellectual elite, schooled in mathematics and philosophy, ruled it. At the top of the political pyramid was a philosopher-king, the wisest and most virtuous product of a state-training program that consumed the better part of his life. Culture was not encouraged in the Republic; dangerous and novel ideas were banned, poets were banished, all music was prohibited except the martial, patriotic type.

What are we to make of a utopia that would encourage Sousa but ban Brahms—a polis that could never have produced a Plato? We must remember that democratic Athens was in decline when Plato wrote. He could not love the polis that had executed his master, nor was he blind to the selfish individualism and civic irresponsibility that afflicted fourth-century Greece. Plato had the wit to recognize that through the intensity of its cultural creativity, and the freedom and breadth of its intellectual curiosity, the polis was burning itself out. Achilles had chosen a short but glorious life; Plato preferred longevity even at the cost of mediocrity, and he designed his Republic to achieve that goal. There would be no Sophists to erode civic virtue, no poets to exalt the individual over the community (or

---

*Jesus would have been denied tenure on the same grounds.

abandon their shields as they fled from battle). Plato's cavalier treatment of the mercantile classes represents a deliberate rejection of the lures of empire. Like a figure on a Grecian urn, his ideal polis would be frozen and rigid—and enduring.

There remains the paradox that this intellectually static commonwealth was to be ruled by philosophers. We tend to think of philosophy as a singularly disputatious subject, but Plato viewed truth as absolute and unchanging. He assumed that all true philosophers would be in essential agreement—that all future thinkers would be Platonists.

This assumption has proven to be resoundingly false, yet Plato's conception of reality has nevertheless exerted an enormous influence on the development of thought. His purpose was to reconcile his belief in a perfect, unchanging universe with the diversity and impermanence of the visible world. He stated that the objects that we perceive through our senses are merely pale, imperfect reflections of ideal models or archetypes that exist in a world invisible to us. For example, we observe numerous individual cats, some black, some yellow, some fat, some skinny. All are imperfect particularizations of an ideal cat existing in the Platonic heaven. Again, we find in the world of the senses many examples of duality: twins, lovers, pairs of jackasses, and so forth, but they merely exemplify, more or less inadequately, the idea of "two" which, in its pure state, is invisible and intangible. We cannot see "two." We can only see two *things*. But—and this is all important—we can *conceive* of "twoness" or abstract duality. Likewise, with sufficient effort, we can conceive of "catness," "dogness," and "rabbitness"—of the archetypal cat, dog, or rabbit. If we could not, so Plato believed, we would have no basis for grouping individual cats into a single category.

In short, the world of phenomena is not the *real* world. The phenomenal world is variegated and dynamic; the real world—the world of archetypes—is clear-cut and static. We can discover this real world through introspection, for knowledge of the archetypes is present in our minds from birth, dimly remembered from a previous existence. (Plato believed in a beforelife as well as in an afterlife.) So the philosopher studies reality not by observing but by thinking.

Plato illustrated this doctrine with a vivid metaphor. Imagine a cave whose inhabitants are chained in such a position that they can never turn toward the sunlit opening but can see only shadows projected against an interior wall. Imagine further that one of the inhabitants (the philosopher) breaks his chains, emerges from the cave, and sees the real world for the first time. He will have no wish to return to his former shadow world, but he will do so nevertheless out of a sense of obligation to enlighten the others. Similarly, the philosopher-king rules the Republic unwillingly through a sense of duty. He would prefer to contemplate reality undisturbed. Yet he alone can rule wisely, for he alone has seen the truth.

Plato's doctrine of ideas has always been alluring to people who seek order and unity, stability and virtue, in a universe that appears fickle and chaotic. Plato declared that the greatest of the archetypes is the idea of the Good, and this notion has had great appeal to people of religious temperament ever since. His theory of knowledge, emphasizing contemplation over observation, is obviously hostile to the method of experimental science, yet his archetypal world is perfectly compatible with the world of the mathematician—the world of pure numbers. Plato drew heavily from the Pythagorean tradition—"God is a mathematician," he once observed—and Platonic thought, like Pythagorean thought, has contributed profoundly to the development of mathematical science. As for philosophy, it developed over the next two thousand years in the shadow of two giants. One of them is Plato; the other, Aristotle, Plato's greatest pupil.

ARISTOTLE (384–322)

Plato founded a school in Athens called the Academy (the source of our word, *academic*). To this school came the young Aristotle, the son of a Greek physician in the service of the king of Macedon. Aristotle remained at the Academy for nearly two decades. Then, after serving at the Macedonian court as tutor to Alexander the Great, he returned to Athens, founded a school of his own (the Lyceum), and wrote most of his books. At length he was condemned by the Athenians for "impiety" and escaped into exile, explaining as he fled that he wished to spare the Athenians from "a second sin against philosophy." He died shortly thereafter, in 322, one year after the death of Alexander. Thus, Aristotle's life spanned the final years of Classical Greece.

Aristotle was a universal scholar. He wrote definitively on a great variety of topics including biology, politics, literature, ethics, logic, physics, and metaphysics. He brought Plato's theory of ideas down to earth by asserting that the archetype exists in the particular—that one can best study the archetypal cat by observing and classifying individual cats. He thus gave scientific observation a much higher priority than Plato had accorded it. Like Hippocrates and Thucydides, but on a much broader scale, Aristotle advocated the painstaking collection and analysis of data. Although his political studies included the designing of an ideal commonwealth, he also investigated and classified the political systems of many existing poleis and demonstrated that several different types were conducive to the good life. His ground-breaking biological studies followed the same method of observation and classification, and he set forth the concepts of genus and species which, with modifications, are still used. His work on physics has been less durable because it was based on an erroneous concept of motion, a fundamental belief in *purpose* as the organizing factor in the material universe, and an emphasis on qualitative rather than quantitative differences (for example, that the heavenly bodies are more perfect than objects on the earth). Mathematics had no genuine role in his system; in general, modern science draws its experimental method from the Aristotelian tradition and its mathematical analysis from the Pythagorean-Platonic tradition.

Aristotle's physics and metaphysics were based on the concept of a single God who was the motive power behind the universe—the unmoved mover and the uncaused cause to which all motion and all causation must ultimately be referred. Hence, Aristotelian thought was able to serve as a philosophical framework for later Islamic and Christian thought. Aristotle's immense significance in intellectual history arises from his having done some of the best thinking up to his time in so many significant intellectual disciplines. It was he who first set forth a systematic logic, who first produced a rigorous, detailed physics, who literally founded biology. A pioneer in observational method, he has been criticized for basing conclusions on insufficient evidence. Even Aristotle was not immune to the tendency toward premature conclusions, yet he collected data as no Greek before him had done. His achievement, considered in its totality, is unique in the history of thought.

Plato and Aristotle represent the apex of Greek philosophy. Both were religious men—both, in fact, were monotheists at heart. But both were dedicated also to the life of reason. Building on a rational heritage that had only begun in the sixth century, both produced philosophical systems of unparalleled sophistication and depth. Their thought climaxed the intellectual revolution that brought such glory and such turmoil to Greece.

Chapter
9

The Culture of the Golden Age

History has never seen anything quite like the cultural creativity of fifth-century Athens. It has been suggested that the Athenians of the golden age were incapable of producing anything ugly or vulgar; every surviving work of art, from the greatest temple to the simplest ornament, was created with unerring taste and assurance. Emotions ran strong and deep, but they were controlled by a sure sense of form that never permitted ostentation yet never degenerated into formalism. The art of the period was an incarnation of the Greek maxim: "nothing in excess"—a perfect embodiment of the taut balance and controlled excitement that we call "the classical spirit."

Classical Greek culture reflected the liberty and dynamism of the polis. Compared to the societies of the Near East, the world of the polis was intense and fluid. Political systems, philosophical concepts, and artistic styles evolved at a furious pace. Aristocracies declined, tyrannies flourished, and democracies emerged in an atmosphere of social change and acute political awareness. The citizens of the Greek poleis recognized that they were a people apart and that what separated them most fundamentally from their predecessors and contemporaries was their freedom. Herodotus describes Greeks as speaking to a Persian official in these words: "A slave's life you understand, but never having tasted liberty you cannot tell whether it be sweet or not. Had you known what freedom is, you would have bidden us fight for it." And the whole Persian War becomes for Herodotus an epic struggle between slavery and freedom.

It is not difficult to understand how Greek citizens, whose freedom exceeded that of any previous civilized people, produced such a dynamic culture. It is less easy to explain the harmony and restraint of Greek classicism, for no people had ever before lived with more intensity and fervor. Herodotus tells us that even the barbaric Scythians lamented the Greek impulse toward frenzy, and a speaker in Thucydides observes that the Athenians "were born into the world to take no rest themselves and to give none to others."

The Greeks stressed the importance of moderation and restraint precisely because these were the qualities most needed by an immoderate, unrestrained people. A degree of cooperation and self-control was essential to the communal life of the polis, and civic devotion acted as a brake on rampant individualism. During its greatest years the polis stimulated individual creativity but directed it toward the welfare of the community. Individualism and civic responsibility achieved a momentary and precarious balance.

The achievement of this equilibrium in the fifth century was a precious but fleeting episode in the evolution of the polis from the aristocratic conservatism of the previous age to the unbridled individualism of the fourth century and thereafter, hastened by the growth of religious doubt and the tendency toward specialization. This process is illustrated in the evolution of Greek art from the delicate, static elegance of the "archaic style" through the serious, balanced classical style of the fifth century to the increasing individualism and naturalism of the late-

Maiden dressed in a Dorian garment, about 530 B.C.; an example of the archaic style (*Marburg – Art Reference Bureau, Acropolis Museum*).

Apoxyomenos (scraper); Roman marble copy probably of bronze original by Lysippus, about 330 B.C., in the style of the golden age (*Vatican Museum*).

classical fourth century. The works of the fifth-century sculptors were idealized human beings—we might almost say Platonic archetypes. The fourth-century sculptors tended to abandon the archetype for the specific and concrete. In short, as Greek life was evolving from civic allegiance to individualism, from traditionalism to self-expression, from aristocracy to democracy, there was a moment when these opposites were balanced—and the moment was frozen and immortalized in some of the finest works of architecture, sculpture, and dramatic literature the world has known.

The golden age of Greece was the golden age of Athens, for the wealth of empire and the ambitious building program of Pericles drew talent from throughout the Greek world. Periclean Athens had a long artistic tradition behind it and a buoyant self-assurance that was born at Marathon, confirmed at Salamis, and heightened by a successful career in imperialism. But the Athenian golden age was expensive to the rest of Greece in both money and talent. Indeed, the Greek polis system at its cultural zenith had already evolved a good distance from the original ideal of the independent self-contained state. Athens was not merely a polis; it was the heart of an empire. And although civic spirit vitalized Athenian culture, imperial trade and tribute paid the bills. The culture of the golden age is unquestionably a polis culture, but it is the culture of a polis in the process of losing its innocence.

The golden age of Pericles rested not only on economic foundations of imperial tribute but on slavery as well. This fact should not be exaggerated—slavery was the basis of most ancient economies—but it cannot be overlooked.

ATHENIAN LIFE

In Periclean Athens, individualism was still strongly oriented toward the polis. One of the basic differences between the daily life of the fifth-century Athenian citizen and that of the modern American is the Athenian's emphasis on public over private affairs. The private lives of even the most affluent Athenian citizens were rigorously simple: their clothing was plain, their homes were modest, their furniture was rudimentary. With the intensification of individualism in the fourth century, private homes became more elaborate, but during the golden age the Athenian's private life was, by our standards, almost as Spartan as the Spartan's.

The austerity of private life was counterbalanced, however, by the brilliant diversity of public life. Under Pericles, imperial Athens lavished its wealth and genius on its own adornment. The great works of art and architecture were dedicated to the

Discobolus (discus thrower); Roman marble copy of bronze original by Myron, a Greek sculptor of the mid-fifth century B.C. (*Vatican Museum*).

polis and its gods. Life was enriched by the pageantry of civic religious festivals, by spirited conversation in the marketplace (the agora), by exercise in elaborate civic gymnasiums complete with baths and dressing rooms, and of course by participation in political affairs. The Greeks socialized the amenities of life; the pursuit of excellence in body and mind, so typical of Greek culture, was carried on in a communal atmosphere. The good life was not the life of the individual but the life of the citizen.

Not everybody in Athens was a citizen. Women, slaves, children, and metics (resident aliens) were all excluded from the privileges of citizenship. Although many metics prospered in business, many slaves were well-treated, and many women had loving husbands, only free Athenian males could participate fully in the life of the polis. Aristotle sought to give rational sanction to this state of affairs by proving (to his own satisfaction) that slaves and women were naturally inferior beings.

The citizen's wife in Periclean Athens remained in the home. She had heavy domestic duties but few social responsibilities and was legally under her husband's control. The parties and festive gatherings of the citizens included no wives but were enlivened by the presence of *hetairai* ("female companions")— high-class prostitutes of good education and free status. The *hetairai* were non-Athenians, often from Ionia, and were celebrated for their wit and charm. Notable among them was an Ionian woman named Aspasia, who owned her own bordello, enjoyed intellectual conversations with Socrates, and became Pericles' mistress. Her name, appropriately, means "welcome."

For Athenian wives, the age of Pericles was far from golden. Their lot is expressed eloquently in one of the tragedies of Euripides:

A man, when he's bored with being at home
Can go out and escape depression
By turning to some friend, or whatever.
But we wives have one soul to look to. They say we lead a safe life at home
While they do battle with the spear.
What imbeciles! I'd rather stand to arms
*Three times than bear one child.**

GREEK DRAMA

The civic culture of the golden age achieved its most remarkable triumphs in drama, architecture, and sculpture. All three illustrate the public orientation of Greek cultural life. Greek tragedy rose out of the worship of Dionysus, as the songs and dances of the worshipers gradually evolved into a formalized drama with

---

*Medea 244–251; tr. Frank J. Frost, *Greek Society*, 2nd ed. (Lexington, Mass., 1980), p. 94. By permission of Frank J. Frost.

actors and a chorus. The sixth-century Athenian tyrant Pisistratus gave vigorous support to the festival of Dionysus, and by the fifth century it had become a great civic institution. Wealthy citizens were expected to finance the productions, and each year a body of civic judges would award prizes to the three best tragedies.

By modern standards the performances were far from elaborate. The most important of them took place in the outdoor Theater of Dionysus that stands to this day on the southern slope of the Acropolis. The chorus sang and danced to a simple musical accompaniment and commented at intervals on the action of the drama. Behind the chorus were low, broad steps on which the actors performed. There were never more than three actors on the stage at one time, and the sets behind them were simple in the extreme. The dramas were based on mythological or historical themes, often dealing with semi-legendary royal families of early Greece, but the playwrights went beyond the realm of historical narrative to probe deeply some of the fundamental problems of morality and religion.

The immense popularity of these stark, profound, uncompromising productions testifies to the remarkable cultural elevation of fifth-century Athens. The citizens who flocked to the Theater of Dionysus constituted a critical and sophisticated audience. Many had themselves participated in the numerous dramas that were constantly being performed both in the city and in the surrounding Attican countryside. It has been estimated that each year some 3000 citizens had the experience of performing in a dramatic chorus, and thousands more had been trained, as a part of the normal Athenian curriculum, in singing, dancing, declamation, and acting. The drama was a central and meaningful element in the life of the polis and serves as an added illustration of the versatility of Athenian citizens during the golden age.

The three great tragedians of fifth-century Athens were Aeschylus, who wrote during the first half of the century; Sophocles, whose productive period covered the middle and later decades of the century; and Euripides, a younger contemporary of Sophocles. All three exemplify the seriousness, order, and controlled tension that we identify as "classical," yet they also illustrate the changes the classical spirit was undergoing. Aeschylus, the first of the three, tended to emphasize traditional values. Deeply devoted to the polis and the Greek religious heritage, he probed with majestic dignity the fundamental relationships of humanity and its gods, the problem of injustice in a righteous universe, and the terrible consequences of overweening pride.

Sophocles was less intellectually rigorous and less traditional than Aeschylus. But he was a supreme dramatic artist with an unerring sense of plot-structure and characterization. His plays treat the most violent and agonizing emotional situations with restraint and sobriety. In Sophocles the classical equilibrium is fully achieved: intense passion under masterful control.

The younger dramatist Euripides displays the logic, the skepticism, and the hard-headed rationalism of the Sophists who were then the rage of Athens. One of his characters makes the audacious statement, "There are no gods in heaven; no, not one!" And Euripides, far more than his predecessors, demonstrated a deep, sympathetic understanding of the hopes and fears, the unpredictability and irrationality, the *individuality* of human nature. Aeschylus' characters were chiefly types rather than individuals; in Sophocles the individual emerges with much greater clarity; but Euripides portrays his characters with unparalleled realism and psychological insight. With the tragedies of Euripides, the new age of skepticism and individualism was dawning.

The depth and power of fifth-century tragedy is exemplified in Sophocles' *Antigone*, which deals with the perennial conflict between individual conscience and public authority. Antigone's brother has betrayed his country and has been killed. Her uncle, the king of Thebes, refuses to permit her brother's burial even though burial was regarded as a sacred duty in the Greek religious tradition. Torn by the conflict between the royal decree and her sense of religious obligation, Antigone defies the king, buries her brother, and is condemned to death. She addresses the king in these words:

> I did not think that your decrees were of such force
> as to override the unwritten and unfailing laws of
> heaven. For their duration is not of today or yester-

day, but from eternity; and no one knows when they were first put forth. And though men rage I must obey those laws. Die I must, for death must come to all. But if I am to die before my time, I'll do it gladly; for when one lives as I do, surrounded by evils, death can only be a gain. So death for me is but a trifling grief, far better than to let my mother's son lie an unburied corpse.

The lighter side of the fifth-century theater is represented by the comic playwright Aristophanes who, taking advantage of the freedom of the Athenian theater, subjected his fellow citizens great and small to merciless ridicule as he exposed the pretensions and follies of imperial Athens during the Peloponnesian War. A product of the age of Socrates and the Sophists, Aristophanes expressed his deep-rooted conservatism by lampooning them. Socrates appears in a comedy called *The Clouds* hanging from a basket suspended in the air so that he could contemplate the heavens at closer range, while his students below studied geology, their noses in the earth and their posteriors upraised toward the sky.

The plays of Aristophanes reflect the political discontent of his audiences. He mocked Athens' leaders with a frankness that would seldom be tolerated by a modern democracy during wartime. The audacity of his criticism illustrates the degree of intellectual freedom that existed in fifth-century Athens. Yet his plays also betray a yearning for the dignity and traditionalism of former years and a disturbing conviction that all was not well.

ARCHITECTURE AND SCULPTURE

Every aspect of fifth-century culture displays the classical spirit of restrained excitement. We find it in Athenian drama where the most violent deeds and passions are presented in an ordered and unified framework. We find it in the history of Thucydides, who treats with dispassionate analysis the impetuous and often childish excesses of the Peloponnesian War. And we find it in the architecture and art of fifth-century Athens: deeply moving yet balanced and controlled.

When Xerxes burned the Acropolis he left the next generation of Athenians with a challenge and an opportunity: to rebuild the temples in the new, classical style—to crown the polis with structures of such perfection as the world had never seen. Athenian imperialism provided the money with which to rebuild, and Pericles, against the opposition of a conservative minority, pursued a lavish policy of civic beautification as a part of his effort to make Athens the cultural center of Hellas. The age of Pericles was therefore a period of feverish public building; its supreme architectural momument was the central temple on the reconstructed Acropolis—the Parthenon. This structure, dedicated to the patron goddess Athena, is the ultimate expression of the classical ideal. It creates its effect not from a sense of fluidity and upward-reaching, as in the medieval Gothic cathedrals and twentieth-century skyscrapers, but from a superb harmony of proportions. Here indeed was "nothing in excess."

The genius of the architects was matched by that of the sculptors who decorated the temples and created the great statues that were placed inside them. The most distinguished of the fifth-century sculptors was Phidias, the master sculptor of the Parthenon, who was responsible either directly or through his helpers for its splendid reliefs. Phidias made a majestic statue of Athena in ivory and gold for the interior of the Parthenon, and a still larger statue of the same goddess which was placed in the open and could be seen by ships several miles at sea.

The work of Phidias and his contemporaries comes at the great moment of classical balance. Their works portray human beings as types, without individual problems or cares, vigorous yet serene, ideally proportioned, and often in a state of controlled tension.

The architecture and sculpture of the Parthenon and its surrounding temples exemplify the synthesis of religious feeling, patriotic dedication, artistic genius, and intellectual freedom that characterized the age of Pericles. It would be pleasant to think of the Athenians of this period enjoying the beauty of these temples that so perfectly express the mood of the age. But such was not the case. The Parthenon, the first of the Acropolis structures to be completed, was not finished until 432, a scant

The Acropolis of Athens (*Alinari—Art Reference Bureau*).

The Parthenon (*Marburg—Art Reference Bureau*).

Head of the Athena Lemnia; after Phidias, fifth century B.C.
(*Alinari—Art Reference Bureau, Civic Museum Bologna*).

year before the outbreak of the Peloponnesian War that ultimately brought Athens to its knees. By 432 the old civic-
religious enthusiasm was already waning. For centuries after,
Greek art would be a living, creative force; indeed, some of its
most celebrated masterpieces were products of these later centuries. But the balanced, confident spirit of Periclean Athens—
the spirit that informed the works of Sophocles and Phidias and
inspired the Parthenon—could never quite be recovered.

Chapter
10
The Hellenistic Age

ALEXANDER THE GREAT

The decline of the polis in the fourth century culminated, as we have seen, in the triumphs of King Philip and the subordination of all Greece to the power of Macedon. In 336 B.C., barely two years after his climactic victory over Athens and Thebes at Chaeronea, Philip of Macedon was murdered as a consequence of a palace intrigue. He was succeeded by his son Alexander, later to be called "the Great."

In his final months Philip had been preparing a large-scale attack against the Persian Empire. His hope was to transform the grudging obedience of the Greek city-states into enthusiastic support by leading a Pan-Hellenic crusade against the traditional enemy of Hellas. Alexander, during a dazzling reign of thirteen years, exceeded his father's most fantastic dreams. Leading his all-conquering armies from Greece to India, he changed the course of the ancient world.

Marble portrait of Alexander the Great: Late Hellenistic.
A break has damaged the nose badly, and the mouth
and chin slightly.

Although only twenty when he inherited the throne, Alexander possessed in the fullest measure the combination of physical attractiveness, athletic prowess, and intellectual distinction that had long been the Greek ideal. He had a godly countenance, the physique of an Olympian athlete, and a penetrating, imaginative mind. He was a magnetic leader who inspired intense loyalty and admiration among his followers, a brilliant general who adapted his tactics and strategy to the most varied circumstances, and an ardent champion of Hellenic culture and the Greek way of life. He was the product of two great teachers:

Aristotle, the master philosopher and universal intellect, and King Philip himself, the best general and most adroit political opportunist of the age. Alexander's turn of mind is symbolized by the two objects that he kept beneath his pillow: the *Iliad* and a dagger.

At first the Greek city-states were restive under Alexander's rule. He quelled their revolts with merciless efficiency, destroying rebellious Thebes and frightening the rest into submission. But there was genuine support for his campaign against the Persian Empire. In the spring of 334 B.C. he led a Greco-Macedonian army of some 40,000 men into Asia Minor, and, during the next 3½ years, won a series of stunning victories over the declining, ramshackle Persian Empire. He freed the Ionian cities from Persian control and conquered the imperial provinces of Syria and Egypt. Then, striking deep into the heart of the Empire, he won a decisive victory over the unwieldy Persian army near Arbela on the Tigris in 331. The triumph at Arbela enabled Alexander to seize the vast imperial treasure, ascend the imperial throne, and bring an end to the dynasty of ancient Persia.

This was a glorious moment for the Greeks. The foe that had so long troubled Hellas was conquered. More than that, the ancient Near East was now under Greek control, open to Greek enterprise, Greek culture, Greek rationalism, and (not to get carried away) Greek exploitation. Alexander's conquest of Persia set the stage for a new epoch—a period known as the *Hellenistic Age* as distinct from the previous *Classical Age.* The Greeks were now the masters of the ancient world, and under their rule a great cosmopolitan culture developed, distinctly Greek in tradition yet transmuted by the influence of the subject oriental civilizations and by the spacious new environment in which the Greeks now lived. The new culture has thus been termed "Hellenistic"—not purely Greek (Hellenic) but "Greek-like."

The spreading of Greek civilization across the Near East was facilitated by Alexander's policy of founding cities in the wake of his conquests and filling them with Greek settlers. These communities, although intended chiefly as military and commercial bases, became islands of Greek culture which often exerted a powerful influence on the surrounding area. Most of them were named, immodestly, after their founder. The greatest of them by far was Alexandria in Egypt, which Alexander established at the mouth of the Nile. Alexandria quickly outstripped the cities of Greece itself to become the commercial metropolis of the Hellenistic world, and before long it had developed a cultural and intellectual life that put contemporary Athens to shame.

No sooner had he ascended the throne of Persia than Alexander began preparations for further campaigns. The final seven years of his life were occupied in conquering the easternmost provinces of the Persian Empire and pushing on into India, impelled by a thirst for conquest and the lure of undiscovered lands. His spirit and ingenuity were taxed to the utmost by the variety of difficulties that he encountered: the rugged mountains of Afghanistan, the hostile stretches of the Indus Valley, fierce armies equipped with hundreds of elephants. At length his own army, its endurance exhausted, refused to go further. Alexander returned to central Persia in 323 where, in the midst of organizing his immense empire, he fell ill and died, perhaps of malaria, at the age of thirty-two.

The empire of Alexander was the greatest that the world had yet seen—more extensive even than the Persian Empire. Wherever he went Alexander adapted himself to the customs of the land. He ruled Egypt as a divine pharaoh and Persia as a Near Eastern despot, demanding that his subjects prostrate themselves in his presence. (His Greek followers objected vigorously to this.) He married the daughter of the last Persian emperor and urged his countrymen to follow his example by taking wives from among the Persian aristocracy. His goal was apparently nothing less than a homogeneous Greco-Oriental empire—a fusion of East and West. To what extent this policy was the product of deliberate calculation, to what extent a consequence of his intoxication with the splendors of the ancient Orient will never be known. But the project was scarcely underway when Alexander died, leaving behind him a sense of loss and bewilderment, and a vast state that nobody but a second Alexander could have held together.

It is a little odd that Alexander's achievements have been so

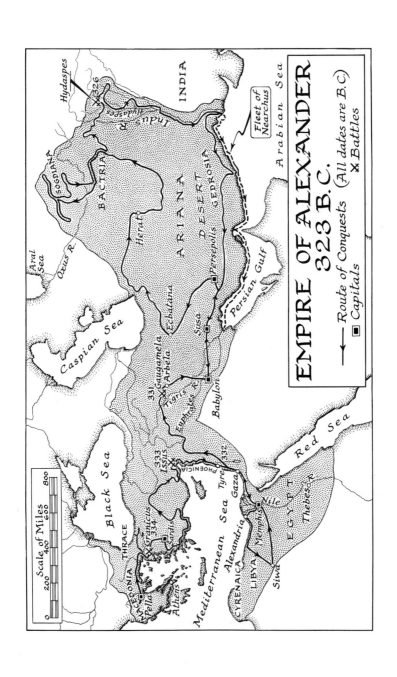

EMPIRE OF ALEXANDER
323 B.C.

→ Route of Conquests (All dates are B.C)
■ Capitals
✗ Battles

Fleet of Nearchus

Arabian Sea

INDIA

Hydaspes
✗326
Hydaspes
INDUS R.

SOGDIANA
BACTRIA
Oxus R.
Aral Sea

Herat
ARIANA
GEDROSIA
DESERT

Caspian Sea

Ecbatana
Susa
Persepolis
Persian Gulf

Gaugamela
✗ 331
Arbela
Tigris R.
Euphrates R.
Babylon

Black Sea

Issus
✗ 1333

Granicus R.
✗ 334
Sardis

THRACE
MACEDONIA
Pella
Athens

PHOENICIA
Tyre
Gaza
Alexandria
Mediterranean Sea
CYRENAICA
LIBYA
Siwa
Memphis
Nile
Thebes
EGYPT
Red Sea

Scale of Miles
0 200 400 600 800

much admired, considering that he devoted himself singlemindedly to ruthless attacks against lands into which he had not been invited. Perhaps it would be unfair to ascribe his enviable historical reputation to the fact that, to some Western tastes, he was much better looking than such later conquerors as Ghengis Khan and Attila the Hun. But the Greeks themselves related the story of a pirate whom Alexander had taken prisoner telling his captor that the difference between them was only one of scale.

THE SUCCESSOR STATES

Alexander's empire was divided among his leading generals, who founded a series of Macedonian dynasties that ruled Greece and most of the ancient Near East until the Roman conquests of the second and first centuries B.C. There was great conflict over the division of the spoils, and for several decades after Alexander's death the political situation remained fluid. But in broad outline the succession went as follows: Ptolemy, one of Alexander's ablest generals, ruled Egypt, establishing the Ptolemaic dynasty that lasted until a Roman army deposed Cleopatra, the last of the Ptolemies, in 30 B.C. From their magnificent capital of Alexandria, the Ptolemies ruled with all the pomp and authority of the most powerful pharaohs, enriching themselves through the tight control that pharaohs had traditionally imposed on the Egyptian economy. Alexandria, with its imposing public buildings, its superb library and museum, its far-flung commerce, and its million inhabitants was the wonder of the age. But elsewhere Egypt remained essentially unchanged.

Northern Syria and most of the remaining provinces of the old Persian Empire fell to another of Alexander's generals, Seleucus, who founded the Seleucid dynasty. The kingdom of the Seleucids was far more heterogeneous and loosely organized than that of the Ptolemies, and as time went on certain of the more self-conscious Near Eastern peoples began to rebel against the Seleucid policy of Hellenization. This was particularly true of the Persians and Jews, who had each produced powerful transcendental religions and resented bitterly the influx of Greek religious thought. Farther to the east, the Parthians, a non-Persian Caspian people, had taken most of the Iranian plateau by the mid-third century. The center of Seleucid power was the city of Antioch in northern Syria, second only to Alexandria in population, wealth, and opulence.

The third important successor state, Macedon, passed to a dynasty known as the Antigonids, whose authority over the Greek poleis to the south was never very firm and whose power was usually inferior to that of the Ptolemies and Seleucids. A number of smaller states also developed out of the imperial wreckage, but the three dominant successor kingdoms were Antigonid Greece, Seleucid Asia, and Ptolemaic Egypt.

THE CHANGE IN MOOD

These huge political agglomerations now replaced the city-states as the characteristic sovereign units of the Greek world. The new environment provided vast opportunities and encouraged a sense of cosmopolitanism that contrasted with the former provincialism of the polis. This was a prosperous age, of vigorous and profitable business activity and successful careers in commerce and banking. But as always, the good life was reserved for the fortunate few. Slavery continued, even increased, and the peasants and urban commoners remained at an economic level of bare subsistence. The typical agrarian unit was no longer the small or middle-sized farm but the large plantation worked by slaves.

The poleis in Greece itself retained throughout the new age a portion of their earlier autonomy. Old civic institutions continued to function and citizens still had a voice in domestic politics. But the Greek peninsula was now an economic backwater, and cities like Athens and Thebes were overshadowed by the new superstates. Ambitious Greeks were lured by opportunity far from their homeland, as they had once been lured to imperial Athens. No longer involved in political affairs or in the intense life of a free community, overseas Greeks found themselves adrift in a wide and bewildering world over which they had little control.

Old Market Woman: Hellenistic realism, second century B.C. (*The Metropolitan Museum of Art, Rogers Fund, 1909*).

The cosmopolitanism of the Hellenistic age was accompanied by a sense of estrangement and alienation, uncertainty, and loneliness. The trend toward individualism, professionalism, and specialization accelerated. The impulse toward realism in literature and art was pushed to its limits. Many Hellenistic artists turned to portraying the tragic and grotesque—ugliness, deformity, agony—often with powerfully effective results. The civic consciousness of the comic playwright Aristophanes in the fifth century gave way to the highly individualized realism of the Hellenistic drawing-room comedy and bedroom farce. The Hellenistic sculptors, on the other hand, produced superb works of art—lacking the serenity and balance of the earlier period, but often surpassing it in psychological depth and emotional impact.

RELIGION AND ETHICS

Hellenic religion, with its traditional civic orientation, was all but transformed in this new age. Ancient bonds and loyalties were broken as many adventurous Greeks were uprooted from their poleis and thrown on their own. The result was a mood of intense individualism which found expression in a variety of religious and ethical ideas stressing personal fulfillment or personal salvation rather than involvement in the community. Individualism and cosmopolitanism went hand in hand, for as the Greeks abdicated spiritually from the polis and retired into themselves, they came to regard all humanity as a multitude of individuals—a universal community in which intelligent Persians, Egyptians, and Jews were no worse than intelligent Greeks. The traditional contrast between Greek and barbarian faded, for it had been the free spirit of the polis that had set the Greek apart, and the polis, in its traditional sense, was now becoming an anachronism. Yet the concept of cosmopolis, the idea of human brotherhood, was too abstract to provide the sense of involvement and orientation that the polis had formerly given. The rootless Greek tended to turn away from the old Olympic gods and seek solace in more personal and potent religious concepts. Hellenistic religion is characterized by a withdrawal from active social participation—a search for sanctuary in a restless, uncertain world.

The Hellenistic age saw a revival of mystery and salvation cults such as Orphism and the worship of Dionysus and Demeter which had always lurked behind the Olympic foreground. And various Near Eastern mystery religions now be-

Laocoön, late second century B.C.; sculpture shows Laocoön and his sons struggling with snakes (*Alinari—Art Reference Bureau, Vatican Museum*).

came popular among the Greeks. Almost all of these were centered on the death and resurrection of a god and the promise of personal salvation. From Egypt came the cult of Osiris who died, was reborn, and now sat in judgment of the dead. From Asia Minor came a version of the ancient and widespread fertility cult of the Great Mother. From Persia, somewhat later, came the cult of Mithras, a variation of Zoroastrianism, which added to the traditional concept of a cosmic struggle between good and evil the idea of a savior-hero who redeemed mankind.

Alongside these and other oriental cults came a revival of neo-Babylonian astrology, of magic, witchcraft, and sorcery. Many ambitious Greeks of the upper class were devoted to the goddess of Fortune who rewarded talent and ambition and brought her worshipers material well-being. The Hellenistic world became a religious melting pot in which a single individual might be a devotee of several cults. Many thoughtful people adopted the idea of "syncretism"—the notion that the gods of different peoples are actually various manifestations of the same god, that Zeus, Osiris, even Yahweh, all symbolize a single divine spirit. (The more orthodox among the Jews found this doctrine abominable.) Religious beliefs and attitudes throughout the Hellenistic world were preparing fertile soil for the later emergence of Christianity.

SKEPTICS, CYNICS, STOICS, AND EPICUREANS

Many Greeks of the post-Classical age turned neither to the old Orphic and Dionysian cults nor to the salvation cults of the Orient but sought to adapt elements of the Hellenic intellectual tradition to the new conditions. One group, the Skeptics, intensified the relativism of the Sophists by denying the possibility of any knowledge whatever, either of people, gods, or nature. The human mind, they maintained, is incapable of apprehending reality (if, indeed, there is any such thing as "reality"), and all beliefs and statements of fact are equally unverifiable. In doubting everything they carried rationalism to its ultimate, self-destructive limit and reflected the profound uncertainty of the new age.

Another group, the Cynics, demonstrated in various forms of eccentric behavior their contempt for conventional piety and patriotism and their rebellion against the hypocrisy that they detected in the lives and attitudes of their contemporaries. Diogenes, the most famous of the Cynics, was a fourth-century dropout who sought integrity in a world of careerists and phonies. He rejected all official and traditional religions, all participation in civic life, marriage, the public games, and the theater. He ridiculed the prestige associated with wealth, power, and reputation and honored instead the simple life of courage, reason, and honesty—a life of virtue—which could best be attained by a rejection of civilization and a return to nature. The person of wisdom and integrity should live like a dog, without pretensions or worldly possessions. Indeed, the very word *cynic* originally meant *canine* or "doglike."

Diogenes wandered the streets begging for his food, a homeless but free man. His bedchamber was a tub outside a temple of the Great Mother; his latrine was the public street. He obeyed no laws, recognized no polis, and became, next to Alexander, the greatest celebrity of his age. He was a colorful symbol of the great Hellenistic withdrawal from the polis into the soul.

The same withdrawal is evident in the two religio-ethical systems that emerged in the fourth century and influenced human thought and conduct for centuries thereafter: Stoicism and Epicureanism. Both were philosophies of resignation that taught believers to fortify their souls against the harshness of life.

Stoicism derives its name from an Athenian civic building, the "Painted Stoa," in which Zeno, the founder of Stoic philosophy, taught his followers.* Zeno stressed, as the Cynics did, the worthlessness of worldly goods and the supreme importance of individual virtue. All people, whether rulers, nobles, artists, or peasants, should pursue their vocations honestly and seriously. The significant thing is not individual accomplishment but individual effort; politics, art, and even farming are ultimately valueless, yet in working at them as best we can, we manifest our virtue. Since virtue is all-important, good Stoics are immune to the vicissitudes of life. They may lose their property; they might even be imprisoned and tortured; but except by their own will they cannot be deprived of their virtue—their only really precious possession. By rejecting the world, Stoics created

---

*The ruins of the Painted Stoa were unearthed in 1981 by a team of archeologists digging in the Athenian Agora.

impenetrable citadels within their own souls. Out of this doctrine there emerged a sense not only of individualism but of
cosmopolitanism; the idea of the polis faded before the wider
Stoic concept of an encompassing human community.

Ultimately the Stoic emphasis on virtue was rooted in a
cosmic vision based on the Greek conception of a rational,
orderly, purposeful universe. Zeno taught that the harmonious
movements of the stars and planets, the growth of complex
plants from simple seeds, all point to the existence of a Divine
Plan that is both intelligent and good. We humans are incapable
of perceiving the details of the Plan as it works in our own lives,
yet by living virtuously and doing our best, we are cooperating
with it. The God of the universe, Zeno assured his followers,
cares about humanity.

Epicurus, whose school was Stoicism's great rival, differed
from Zeno both in his concept of human ethics and in his vision
of the universe. He taught that people should seek happiness
rather than virtue. Yet happiness to the Epicureans was not the
pursuit of thrills and euphoria, but rather a quiet, balanced life.
The life of the drunkard is saddened by countless hangovers,
the life of the swinger by countless emotional complications.
Happiness is best achieved not by chasing pleasures but by
living simply and unobtrusively, being kind and affectionate to
one's friends, learning to endure pain when it comes, and
avoiding needless fears. In short, good Epicureans did not differ
noticeably from good Stoics in actual behavior, for Stoic virtue
was the pathway to Epicurean happiness. But the Epicureans
rejected the optimistic Stoic doctrine of divine purpose.
Epicurus followed the teachings of the atomists in viewing the
universe not as a great hierarchy of cosmic spheres centering on
the earth, but as a multiplicity of atoms, much the same one
place as another. Our world is not the handiwork of God, but a
chance configuration. The gods, if they exist, care nothing for
us, and we ought to draw from this fact the comforting conclusion that we need not fear them.

Epicureanism even more than Stoicism was a philosophy of
withdrawal. It was a wise, compassionate teaching that sought
to banish fear, curb passions, and dispel illusions. Its doctrine of
happiness was too bland to stir the millions and convert

empires, but it gave solace and direction, during the remaining centuries of antiquity, to an influential minority of wise and sensitive people.

HELLENISTIC SCIENCE

In the Hellenistic age, Greek science reached maturity. The inspired guesswork of the earlier period gave way to a rigorous and highly creative professionalism. Hellenistic scientists followed and improved upon Aristotle's example, collecting and sifting data with great thoroughness before framing their hypotheses.

Alexandria was the center of scientific thought in this age. Here the Ptolemies built and subsidized a great research center—the Museum of Alexandria—and collected a library of unprecedented size and diversity containing some half-million papyrus rolls. At Alexandria and elsewhere, science and mathematics made rapid strides as Greek rationalism encountered the rich, amorphous heritage of Near Eastern astrology, medical lore, and practical mathematics. The fruitful medical investigations of Hippocrates' school were carried on and expanded by Hellenistic physicians, particularly in Alexandria. Their pioneer work in the dissection of human bodies enabled them to discover the nervous system, to learn a great deal about the brain, heart, and arteries, and to perform a variety of new surgical operations. In mathematics, Euclid organized plane and solid geometry into a systematic, integrated body of knowledge. Archimedes of Syracuse did brilliant original work in both pure and applied mathematics, discovering specific gravity, experimenting successfully with levers and pulleys to lift tremendous weights, and coming very close to the invention of calculus.

The wide-ranging military campaigns of Alexander and the subsequent cultural interchange between large areas of the ancient world led to a vast increase in Greek geographical knowledge. Eratosthenes, the head of the Alexandrian Library in the later third century, produced the most accurate and thorough world maps that had yet been made, complete with lines of longitude and latitude and climatic zones. He recognized that the earth was a sphere and was even able to determine its circumference with an error of less than 1%. He did this by measuring the altitude of the sun at different latitudes and calculating from this data the length of degrees of latitude on the earth's surface. Once that was known, Eratosthenes was able to determine the earth's 360-degree circumference by simple multiplication.

The same painstaking accuracy and dazzling ingenuity marks the work of the Hellenistic astronomers. Aristarchus of Samos suggested that the earth rotated daily on its axis and revolved yearly around the sun. This heliocentric hypothesis is a startling anticipation of modern astronomical conclusions, but Aristarchus' erroneous assumption that the earth's motion around the sun was uniform and circular rendered his system inaccurate. Aristarchus' theory was never widely accepted because it failed to explain the precise astronomical observations then being made at Alexandria, and because it violated the hallowed doctrine of an earth-centered universe. Later, the great Hellenistic astronomer Hipparchus developed a complex system of circles and subcircles centered on the earth, which accounted exceedingly well for the observed motions of the sun and moon. Hipparchus' ingenious system, expanded and perfected by the Alexandrian astronomer Ptolemy in the second century A.D., represents antiquity's final word on the subject—a comprehensive geometrical model of the universe that, although it later proved incorrect, corresponded satisfactorily to the best observations of the day. And it should be remembered that a scientific hypothesis must be judged not by some objective standard of rightness or wrongness but by its success in accounting for and predicting observed phenomena. By this criterion the Ptolemaic system stands as one of the impressive triumphs of Greek thought.

THE HELLENISTIC LEGACY

Greek culture exerted a fundamental influence on the Roman Empire, the Byzantine and Muslim civilizations, and the medieval West; but it did so largely in its Hellenistic form. The conclusions of the Hellenistic philosophers and scholars tended to be accepted by the best minds of later ages, but the Hellenistic spirit of free inquiry and intellectual daring was not matched until the sixteenth and seventeenth centuries. There is something remarkably modern about the Hellenistic world with its confident scientists, its cosmopolitanism, its materialism, its religious diversity, its trend toward increasing specialization, its large-scale business activity, and its sense of drift and disorientation. But the Hellenistic economic organization, regardless of superficial similarities, was vastly different from ours. Based on human slavery rather than machines, it provided only a tiny fraction of the population with the benefits of its commercial prosperity. The great majority remained servile, illiterate, and impoverished.

Still, the upper classes throughout the Mediterranean world and the Near East were exposed to Greek culture and the Greek language, and the Greeks themselves were deeply influenced by Oriental thought. From Syria, Asia Minor, and the Nile Valley to Magna Graecia in the West, a common culture was developing with common ideas and common gods. The way was being paved for the political unification of the Mediterranean world under the authority of Rome, and its spiritual unification under the Christian Church. Alexander's dream of a homogeneous Greco-Oriental world was gradually coming into being. But had Alexander foreseen the consequences of his handiwork—the conquest of Hellas by an Italian city and a Near Eastern faith—he might well have chosen to spend his days in seclusion.

Suggested Readings

GENERAL WORKS

Among the many textbooks on ancient Greece the following are particularly recommended: Anthony Andrewes, *The Greeks* (rev. ed., 1978); M.I. Finley, *The Ancient Greeks* (rev. ed., 1977); Frank J. Frost, *Greek Society* (rev. ed., 1980); Peter Green, *Ancient Greece: An Illustrated History* (1979); and H.D.F. Kitto, *The Greeks* (rev. ed., 1963). Other works of a general nature include M.T.W. Arnheim, *Aristocracy in Greek Society* (1977), covering the period from Mycenae to Alexander; and M.I. Finley, *Ancient Slavery and Modern Ideology* (1980), a short, hard-headed account of Greco-Roman slavery and modern misconceptions of it.

CRETE, MYCENAE, AND THE DARK AGE

John Chadwick, *The Decipherment of Linear B,* 2nd ed., (1967). Discusses the achievement of Michael Ventris in cracking the code, and the new world that it disclosed.

John Chadwick, *The Mycenaean World* (1976). A fine, recent overview by a pioneering scholar, stressing social and economic history.

M.I. Finley, *The World of Odysseus* (rev. ed., 1977). A penetrating work of synthesis.

J. Walter Graham, *The Palaces of Crete* (1961). The best treatment of Minoan buildings.

R.W. Hutchinson, *Prehistoric Crete* (1962). A fine general account of Minoan civilization.

William A. McDonald, *Progress into the Past: The Rediscovery of Mycenaean Civilization* (1967). A valuable treatment of modern scholarship and archeology.

Alan E. Samuel, *The Mycenaeans in History* (1966). A lively, concise, well-illustrated narrative of the Mycenaeans from

Neolithic times to the flowering of their culture in the late Bronze Age.

Chester Starr, *The Origins of Greek Civilization, 1100–650 B.C.* (1961). A major work of synthesis demonstrating a firm grasp of both literary and archeological evidence.

THE RISE OF CLASSICAL GREECE

Anthony Andrewes, *The Greek Tyrants* (rev. ed., 1963). Concise, yet probably the best account of the age of the tyrants.

J. Boardman, *The Greeks Overseas* (1964). An expert treatment of the colonization movement.

W.G. Forrest, *A History of Sparta* (1969). A short but exemplary history covering the period 950–192 B.C.

Oswyn Murray, *Early Greece* (1980). A social and economic history from the close of the Mycenaean era to the Persian Wars.

Carl Roebuck, *Ionian Trade and Colonization* (1959). Excellent scholarship; written for advanced students and scholars.

Raphael Sealey, *A History of the Greek City States, 700–338 B.C.* (1976). Emphasizes problems in interpreting the evidence.

Chester Starr, *The Economic and Social Growth of Early Greece, 800–500 B.C.* (1977). An astute analysis that places Greece in its eastern Mediterranean setting.

THE ZENITH AND DECLINE OF CLASSICAL GREECE

C.M. Bowra, *Periclean Athens* (1971). A skillful work of synthesis.

A.R. Burn, *Pericles and Athens* (1962). The best single treatment of Pericles.

Robert Flacelière, *Daily Life in Greece at the Time of Pericles* (1965). Translated from the French, this is an exemplary study of Athenian education, social structure, and everyday life.

Russell Meiggs, *The Athenian Empire* (1972). Explores the motives underlying fifth-century Athenian imperialism.

Sarah B. Pomeroy, *Goddesses, Whores, Wives, and Slaves: Women in Classical Antiquity* (1975). The most sophisticated account of women in contemporary literature and social reality.

R.E. Wycherley, *The Stones of Athens* (1978). Lively, nontechnical essays reconstructing the topography and buildings of Athens in the fifth and fourth centuries B.C.

THOUGHT, LITERATURE, AND ART

The best approach to Greek literature is through the original writings themselves. Homer's *Iliad* and *Odyssey* have often been translated; for the *Iliad*, I suggest the Richmond Lattimore translation, and for the *Odyssey*, the translation by Robert Fitzgerald. Hesiod's *Works and Days* is available in several translations. For the lyric poets see J.M. Edmonds, tr., *Lyra Graeca* (1963). I prefer A. de Selincourt's translation of Herodotus' *The Histories*, and Richard Crawley's translation of Thucydides' *History of the Peloponnesian War*. Xenophon's important history, *The Persian Expedition*, has been best translated by Rex Warner. Plutarch's *Rise and Fall of Athens* includes biographies of nine Greeks who determined the course of Greek history around the period of the Peloponnesian War, written by a Greek-speaking Roman citizen of the early second century A.D. And Moses I. Finley, in his *Greek Historians*, has edited and translated much of Herodotus, Thucydides, Xenophon, and Polybius.

For Greek philosophy, too, the original writings are recommended: Hugh Tredennick, ed. and tr., *The Last Days of Socrates*, presents four dialogues of Plato that cast particular light on the end of Socrates' career. *The Portable Plato*, ed. Scott Buchanan and tr. Benjamin Jowett, provides well-chosen samples. For Aristotle, see Benjamin Jowett and Thomas Twining, tr., *Aristotle's Politics and Poetics*.

C.M. Bowra, *Landmarks in Greek Literature* (1966). Sensitive, perceptive introductions to the major works.

F.M. Cornford, *Before and After Socrates* (1950). A short, lucid account of Greek thought from the Ionians through Aristotle.

H.D.F. Kitto, *Greek Tragedy* 3rd ed., (1961). The classic work on fifth-century tragic drama.

A.W. Lawrence, *Greek Architecture* (1957). Still the best introduction.

J.J. Pollitt, *Art and Experience in Classical Greece* (1972). A sympathetic, thought-provoking interpretation.

THE HELLENISTIC AGE

Alexander the Great has attracted numerous modern biographers, most of them sympathetic but not all. He emerges as a hero in W.W. Tarn, *Alexander the Great* (1948), but less so in A.R. Burn, *Alexander and the Hellenistic World* (rev. ed., 1962). J.R. Hamilton, in his *Alexander the Great* (1973), sees Alexander as ruthlessly ambitious. For more balanced interpretations, see Robin Lane-Fox, *Alexander the Great* (1974), and Mary Renault, *The Nature of Alexander* (1975)—both beautifully written—and, best of all, Peter Green, *Alexander the Great* (1974).

Marshall Clagett, *Greek Science in Antiquity* (rev. ed., 1971). A lucid treatment by a major historian of science.

P.M. Fraser, *Ptolemaic Alexandria* (1972). Very long and very good.

A.A. Long, *Hellenistic Philosophy* (1974). The best general account.

W.W. Tarn and G.T. Griffith, *Hellenistic Civilization* (rev. ed., 1961). The classic account of the post-classical age.

F.W. Walbank, *The Hellenistic World* (1981). A short, skillful survey of Hellenistic politics and culture from the death of Alexander to the Roman conquest of Greece.

C. Bradford Welles, *Alexander and the Hellenistic World* (1970). An excellent account stressing social and economic history.

PART
3
ROME

Chapter
11
The Rise of Rome

CARTHAGE AND MAGNA GRAECIA

Had Alexander lived to middle age instead of dying at thirty-two he might well have led his conquering armies westward into Italy, Sicily, and North Africa. There he would have encountered three vigorous cultures: Carthage, the city-states of Magna Graecia, and the rapidly expanding republic of Rome.

Carthage was originally a Phoenician commercial colony, but its strategic location on the North African coast, just south of Sicily, gave it a stranglehold on the western Mediterranean. It soon developed an extensive commercial empire of its own and far outstripped the Phoenician homeland in power and wealth. Carthage established a number of commercial bases in western Sicily which brought it face-to-face with the Greek city-states that dominated the eastern sections of the island.

The Greek poleis of Sicily and southern Italy, known collectively as Magna Graecia, were products of the age of Greek colonization in the eighth and seventh centuries. Their political evolution ran parallel to that of the city-states in Greece; they experienced the same tensions between aristocratic, oligarchic, and democratic factions and the same intense cultural creativity. And like Old Greece, Magna Graecia was disturbed by intercity warfare. By Alexander's time the Sicilian polis of Syracuse had long been the leading power of the area, but the smaller poleis guarded their independence jealously. Real unification was delayed until the Roman conquests of the third century brought these Greek cities under the sway of a common master.

EARLY ROME

The rise of Rome from an inconsequential central-Italian village to the mastery of the ancient Mediterranean world is one of history's supreme success stories. The process was slow as compared with the dazzling imperialistic careers of Persia and Macedon, but it was far more lasting. There was nothing meteoric about the serious, hard-headed Romans—they built slowly and well. Their great military virtue was not tactical brilliance but stubborn endurance; they lost many battles but from their beginnings to the great days of the Empire they never lost a war. Since it was they who ultimately provided the ancient world with an enduring and all-encompassing political framework, students of history have always been fascinated by the development of Roman political institutions. Rome's greatest contributions were in the realm of law, government, and imperial organization. In its grasp of political realities lay the secret of its triumphant career.

The beginnings of Roman history are obscure. It seems likely that by about 750 B.C. settlers were living in huts on the Palatine Hill near the Tiber River. Gradually, several neighboring hills were settled, and around 600 these various settlements joined together to form the city-state of Rome.

The strategic position of this cluster of hills, fifteen miles inland on one of Italy's greatest rivers, was of enormous importance to Rome's future growth. Ancient ocean-going ships could sail up the Tiber to Rome but no farther, while at the same time Rome was the lowest point at which the river could be bridged easily. Hence Rome was a key river-crossing and road junction and also, at least potentially, a seaport. It was at the northern limit of a fertile agricultural district known us Latium whose rustic inhabitants, the Latins, gave their name to the Latin language. North of Rome lay the district of Etruria (roughly the modern Tuscany)—a more urbanized region whose ruling class, the Etruscans, shaped the culture of early Rome.

Etruscan civilization flourished in central Italy between the eighth and fifth centuries B.C. in an assortment of independent hilltop towns and cities sharing a common culture. Scholars disagree as to whether the Etruscans arose in place or migrated into Etruria from elsewhere (Asia Minor has been suggested). Their culture bears marks of Greek and Near Eastern influence but is highly distinctive nonetheless. They left no literature, and their language, although employing a Greek alphabet, differs so sharply from other languages of the ancient world that scholars have had only limited success in deciphering it.

The Etruscans were skilled engineers who equipped their cities with well-designed drainage systems. They grew wealthy from the abundance of metals within their hills—tin, copper, iron, gold—and wrought them into a marvelous variety of objects, from graceful bronze statues to dental braces. Their remarkable works of art—bronzes, frescoes, decorated urns—disclose a vivacious, pleasure loving civilization of great originality.

It was in Etruscan form that Greek civilization made its first impact on Rome. The Romans adopted the Greek alphabet in its Etruscan version, and perhaps through Etruscan inspiration they organized themselves into a city-state, thereby gaining an inestimable advantage over the numerous half-civilized tribes in the region between Etruria and Magna Graecia. During much of the sixth century, Rome was ruled by kings of Etruscan background whose talented and aggressive leadership made the Romans an important power among the peoples of Latium. The community grew in strength and wealth, and an impressive temple to the Roman god Jupiter was built in Etruscan style atop one of the hills.

CHRONOLOGY OF THE ROMAN EMPIRE

All Dates B.C.

753	Traditional date for Rome's founding
c. 616–509	Etruscan kings rule Rome
c. 450	Twelve Tables
367	Plebeians eligible for consulship
287	Loss of Senate's veto power over plebiscites
265	Rome controls all Italy south of the Po
264–241	First Punic War
218–201	Second Punic War
149–146	Third Punic War
146	Macedonia becomes Roman dependency
133	Tribunate of Tiberius Gracchus
123–122	Tribunate of Gaius Gracchus
121	Gaius Gracchus killed
107	Marius reorganizes military recruitment
83–80	Sulla re-establishes republican constitution
60–44	Caesar a dominant force in Roman politics
43	Cicero killed

THE EMERGENCE OF THE ROMAN REPUBLIC

About 509 B.C. the Roman aristocracy succeeded in overthrowing its Etruscan king, transforming Rome from a monarchy into an aristocratic republic. The king was replaced by two magistrates known as consuls, who were elected annually from the membership of the aristocratic Senate and governed with its advice. The consuls exercised their authority in the name of the Roman people but in the interests of the upper classes. The governing elite was composed of wealthy landowners known as patricians who defended their prerogatives zealously against the encroachments of the lower classes—the plebeians or plebs. Plebeian-patrician intermarriage was prohibited, and for a time the plebeians were almost entirely without political rights.

But step by step the plebeians improved their condition and expanded their role in the government. They began by organizing themselves into a kind of private corporation known as the Council of Plebs. They elected representatives called tribunes to be their spokesmen and represent their interests before the patrician-controlled Roman government. The tribunes acquired the remarkable power of vetoing, in the name of the plebeians, measures issuing from any organ of government. Moreover, anyone violating the sanctity of a tribune's person was to be punished by death. Under the leadership of their tribunes the plebeians were able to act as a unit and to make their strength felt. On at least one occasion, in the midst of a military emergency, they seceded as a body from the Roman state, leaving the patrician army officers with no troops to lead.

In about 450 B.C. the Romans took the important step of committing their legal customs to writing. The result was Rome's first law code—the Twelve Tables. By later standards these laws were harsh (defaulting debtors, for example, suffered capital punishment or were delivered up for sale abroad), but they had the effect of protecting individual plebeians from the capricious authority of the patrician consuls. The Twelve Tables are exceedingly significant as the first great landmark in the evolution of Roman law.

Having gained a measure of legal protection, the plebeians next sought additional farmlands for themselves. The Romans habitually annexed a portion of the territory of conquered peoples, and with such military successes as the capture of the rich Etruscan city of Veii early in the fourth century, the Senate was persuaded to distribute this land to plebeians, both singly and in groups. By providing lands to a growing Roman population, this policy removed some of the economic basis of plebeian discontent.

In time, resolutions (plebiscites) passed by the Council of Plebs came to be accepted as law unless vetoed by the Senate. Intermarriage was now allowed between the two orders, the enslavement of Roman citizens for debt was abolished, and a law of 367 B.C. opened the consulship itself to plebeians. At the same time, or shortly afterwards, it was stipulated that at least one consul must always be a plebeian. In the years that followed plebeians became eligible for all offices of state. Finally, by a law of 287 B.C., the Council of Plebs won the right to have its plebiscites binding on the entire state without being subject to senatorial veto. This was a most remarkable privilege, comparable to the AFL-CIO legislating for the whole American citizenry.

Nevertheless, the rise of the plebs by no means transformed Rome into an egalitarian democracy. The most powerful of the Roman citizens continued to control their state through a client-patron system that dated back to Rome's earliest times. Like the bosses in American cities, wealthy Romans took large numbers of "clients" under their protection, seeing to their economic and legal needs and receiving political support in return. Through their clients, powerful patrons could exercise indirect yet decisive control of Rome's many assemblies and offices, including the Council of Plebs itself.

Meanwhile, the traditional domination by the patricians had gradually given way to a more subtle domination by a new nobility of wealthy, office-holding plebeian and patrician families. According to Roman custom, a family became "noble" when one of its members was elected as a consul, so once the patricians lost their monopoly on the consulship it became possible for politically active plebeians to enter the nobility. During the fifth and fourth centuries, moreover, a number of plebeian families had accumulated extensive estates, and some of them began to rival patricians in wealth and political influence. Rich plebeians now became patrons themselves, with numerous clients of their own. More and more, the plebeian tribunes tended to be drawn from wealthy and "noble" families. By 287—when plebiscites acquired the force of law—the old division between patrician and plebeian was no longer important. The new patrician-plebeian nobility had become Rome's ruling class.

The machinery of Roman republican government was complex and changing. It included numerous civic officials with various titles and responsibilities and several different legislative assemblies, the most important of which were the Centuriate Assembly and the Tribal Assembly—the latter an official body patterned after the plebeians' private Council of Plebs. Both the Centuriate and Tribal Assemblies were made up of the entire Roman citizenry, but each had its own distinctive function and organization. Both of them reflected the domination of the nobles.

The Centuriate Assembly was divided into 193 groups known

as "centuries," each with a single vote. These centuries were distributed according to socioeconomic class, with the richest classes controlling a majority of the centuries. Of the 193 centuries, 98 were allotted to citizens with considerable property, whereas the masses of citizens without any property whatever (the "proles") were lumped into one century, with one vote. Since the richest centuries voted first, and since balloting ceased as soon as a majority was reached, the lesser classes sometimes had no voice at all in the Centuriate Assembly.

The Tribal Assembly was likewise dominated by propertied families, though less directly. Its members were organized by districts known as "tribes" (the Roman citizenry had traditionally been divided into tribal groups: originally about 20, later 35). Each tribe had a single vote, and although the tribes consisted largely of poorer citizens, the noble families were able to influence the Tribal Assembly through their clients. Four of the tribes were urban and thirty-one were rural, and the difficulty of coming in from the countryside resulted in the thirty-one rural votes being controlled by the nobility and the clients they brought with them.

The nobility was thus able to influence both the Centuriate Assembly and the Tribal Assembly, but its primary instrument of power was the Senate. Originally composed of the heads of important families who acted as advisors to the kings, the Senate in the Republic came to be made up of former holders of civic offices, and the senators therefore constituted an impressive reservoir of political talent and experience. Strictly speaking, the Senate was still merely an advisory body, yet because of the unrivaled prestige of its members its actual power far exceeded that of any other organ in the Roman state. Many wealthy plebeians entered the Senate once the civic offices were opened to their order, taking their places alongside the patricians. Thereafter the Senate came to be dominated by an inner core of patrician-plebeian noble families.

Thus, the new nobility retained in practice the control over Roman politics that in theory belonged to all citizens. Nevertheless, there was no shortage of dispute inside the Senate and assemblies since Romans seldom voted on purely economic grounds. And the inclusion of the lesser orders in Roman governance, however limited, stands as a tribute to Rome's political realism. Across the years between the beginning of the Republic and the law on plebiscites, the plebeians won important political powers without the necessity of a major insurrection. Much Roman blood was spilled on battlefields but relatively little on the city's streets. The willingness to settle internal conflicts by compromise—the ability of the patricians to bend before the winds of social change—preserved in Rome a sense of cohesiveness and a spirit of civic commitment without which the conquests would have been impossible.

THE CAREER OF CONQUEST

Civic commitment was a hallmark of the early Romans. Devoted to the numerous gods of city, field, and hearth, they were hard working, respectful of tradition, obedient to civil and military authority, and dedicated to the welfare of the state. The backbone of Old Rome was the small, independent farmer who worked long and hard to raise crops and remained always vigilant against raids by tribesmen from the surrounding hills. To people such as these life was intensely serious. Their stern sobriety and rustic virtues were exaggerated by Roman moralists looking back nostalgically from a later, more luxurious age, but there can be little doubt that the tenacious spirit and astonishing military success of early republican Rome owed much to the discipline and steadfastness of these citizen-farmers. As triumph followed triumph, as the booty of war flowed into Rome from far and wide, the character of its citizenry inevitably suffered; one of the great tragic themes of Roman history is the gradual erosion of social morality by wealth and power—and by the gradual expansion of huge slave-operated estates at the expense of the small farmer. But long before this process was complete the empire had been won.

The expulsion of the last Etruscan king in about 509 B.C. was followed by a period of retrenchment during which the Romans fought for their lives against the attacks of neighboring tribes. In time an alliance was formed between Rome and the communities of Latium in which Rome gradually assumed the role of senior partner. Hostile tribes were subdued by long, agonizing effort. After 400 B.C. the Etruscan cities, unwilling to unite for their mutual defense, fell one by one under Roman control.

The Romans were usually generous with the Italian peoples whom they conquered, allowing them a good measure of internal self-government, and were therefore generally successful in retaining their allegiance. In time, if a conquered people proved loyal, they might hope to be granted Roman citizenship. In this fashion Rome was able to construct an empire far more cohesive and durable than that of Periclean Athens. (Neither Pericles nor any of his contemporaries could have conceived of granting citizenship to non-Athenians.) Gradually, the Roman conquests gained momentum. Battles were often lost—Rome itself was sacked in 387 B.C. by an army of Gauls from the north—but the Romans brushed off their defeats and pressed on. By 265 B.C. all Italy south of the Po Valley was under their control. The Etruscan cities had all passed into Roman hands. Even the Greek cities of Sicily acknowledged Roman supremacy. Now, midway through the third century, Rome took its place alongside Carthage and the three great Hellenistic successor states as one of the leading powers of the Mediterranean world.

Carthage and Rome stood face to face. In 264, a dispute over a Sicilian city initiated the first of three savage conflicts known as the Punic Wars (after Poenus, the Latin word for Phoenician or Carthaginian). Rome was now forced to build a navy and take to the sea. The wars, especially the first two, were long and bitter. Rome lost numerous battles, scores of ships, and warriors and sailors by the hundreds of thousands. During the Second Punic War (218–201 B.C.) the armies of the masterly Carthaginian general Hannibal swept back and forth across Italy winning victory after victory, and only the dogged determination of the Romans and the loyalty of their subject-allies saved the state from extinction. But the Romans hung on, always managing to win the last battle. At the conclusion of the Third Punic War in 146 B.C., Carthage was in ruins and its far-flung territories in Africa, Sicily, and Spain were in Roman hands.

In the meantime Rome was drawn almost inadvertently into

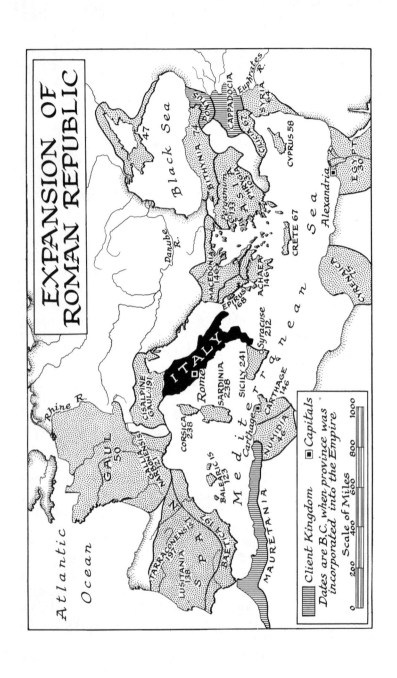

EXPANSION OF ROMAN REPUBLIC

Atlantic Ocean

Rhine R.

Danube R.

Black Sea

GAUL 50

CISALPINE GAUL 191

NARBONENSIS 121

SPAIN

TARRACONENSIS 197

LUSITANIA 138

BAETICA

BALEARIC 123

CORSICA 238

SARDINIA 238

ITALY

Rome

SICILY 241

Carthage CARTHAGE 146

NUMIDIA 46

MAURETANIA

Mediterranean Sea

EPIRUS 168

MACEDONIA 146

ACHAEA 146

Syracuse 212

Tyrrhenian Sea

Pergamum 133

ASIA 133

BITHYNIA 74

PONTUS 65

CAPPADOCIA

GALATIA

PHRYGIA

CILICIA 67

SYRIA 64

Euphrates

CRETE 67

CYPRUS 58

Alexandria

EGYPT 30

CYRENAICA

Client Kingdom ▪ Capitals

Dates are B.C. when province was
incorporated into the Empire

Scale of Miles

0 200 400 600 800 1000

the rivalries among the Hellenistic kingdoms of the eastern Mediterranean. Ptolemaic Egypt, Seleucid Asia, Antigonid Macedon, and the several smaller Greek states had long been at one another's throats; Rome's victories over Carthage increased its power to the point where it was stronger than any one of them. Greek states frequently sought Roman aid against their enemies, and more often than not the Romans gave the requested support to maintain the balance of power in the east and to prevent any one Greek kingdom from becoming dangerously strong.

Rome entered the Greek world more as a pacifier than as a conqueror. But eventually the Romans tired of this endless refereeing and remained to rule. During the second century almost all the Hellenistic world fell either directly or indirectly under Roman control. Rome won a decisive victory over the Seleucids in 189 B.C. It conquered Macedon in 168 B.C. In 146 it demolished the ancient Peloponnesian city of Corinth and transformed Greece into a dependency under the authority of the Roman governor of Macedon. The remaining Hellenistic kingdoms were now overshadowed and had no choice but to bow to Rome's leadership. In time, they all became Roman provinces.

Rome followed no blueprint for conquest—indeed many leading Romans were isolationists who would have preferred to remain aloof from the Greek east—but the political conditions of the Hellenistic states exerted a magnetic attraction that proved irresistible. As the second century drew toward a close, Rome was the master of the Mediterranean world. There now arose the baffling problem of adapting a government designed to rule a city-state to the needs of an empire.

SOCIAL AND POLITICAL CHANGES: 264 TO 146 B.C.

The years of the three Punic Wars witnessed a transformation in the structure and spirit of Rome itself. These changes can be attributed partly to the intoxicating effect of unimagined wealth and military success that gradually undermined the old civic virtue and encouraged a mood of arrogance and materialism. More specifically, as Rome was conquering the Greek world it was falling increasingly under the influence of Hellenistic culture. Roman writers such as Cato the Elder lamented that Roman soldiers were corrupted by the luxuries of eastern Mediterranean lands. Ultimately, Greece was perhaps the victor after all. The full tide of Hellenistic skepticism and individualism, that had earlier undermined allegiance to the Greek polis, now began its corrosive work on Roman conservatism and civic dedication.

As in Greece, the effects of this process were both good and bad. What Rome lost in civic virtue it gained in cultural and intellectual depth, for prior to its Hellenization, Rome was almost totally lacking in high culture. The Stoic notion of universal brotherhood was a singularly appropriate philosophy for a great empire, and it was a fortunate thing for the conquered peoples that in later years so many Roman statesmen became Stoics. But with Greek art, literature, and learning came the disquieting Hellenistic feeling of drift and alienation, aggravated by the shift from family farms to plantations.

Both Carthage and the Hellenistic successor states had emphasized the large plantation over the small independent farm, and the Romans now followed their example. The conquests were bringing vast wealth and hordes of slaves into the hands of the Roman senatorial class, whose members regarded commerce and industry as sordid occupations and were constrained by the strongest of social pressures to invest only in land (in 218 B.C. a law was passed forbidding senators to engage in trade and moneylending). Accordingly, most of central and southern Italy was now converted into huge farms known as *latifundia,* worked by slaves and operated according to the latest Carthaginian and Hellenistic techniques of large-scale farming. Where the small farms had produced grain, the *latifundia* concentrated on the more lucrative production of wine and olive oil or the raising of sheep. The small farmers, whose energy and devotion had built the Roman Empire, were subjected to such heavy military demands that they found it increasingly difficult to maintain their farms. Their numbers were significantly reduced by continuous military conscription for overseas conquests. Many of those who remained sold out to *latifundia* owners and moved into the cities, especially Rome itself, where they were joined by multitudes of penniless immigrants and transformed into a chronically unemployed mob. In later years their riots terrorized the government; their hunger and boredom eventually gave rise to the custom of subsidized food and free entertainment of an increasingly sadistic sort—"bread and circuses."

While Rome was engaged in its struggle with Carthage, important changes were occurring in the social structure of the Roman elite. With the acceleration of commerce, a new, non-noble class of merchants, landowners, and public contractors was developing that in time acquired such wealth as to rival the old nobility. This new class came to be known as the equestrian order because the wealth of its members enabled them to serve in the Roman army as cavalry rather than infantry. The equestrian class was effectively excluded from the Senate. Fundamentally apolitical except in instances when their own interests were at stake, the equestrians were content to share with the nobility the rising living standards resulting from Roman military triumphs and increased contact with the Hellenistic world. As the equestrians and nobles came to live in increasing luxury, the gap between rich and poor steadily widened, and the pressures of social unrest began to threaten the traditional stability of Roman civilization.

Meanwhile the Roman government, which had earlier acted with restraint toward its subject allies in Italy, was proving incapable of governing justly its newly acquired overseas territories. Most of Rome's non-Italian holdings were organized as provinces ruled by aristocratic Roman governors and exploited by Roman tax gatherers. Governor and tax gatherer often worked in partnership to bleed the provinces for personal advantage. The grossest kinds of official corruption were tolerated by the Roman courts of law, whose aristocratic judges hesitated to condemn dishonest officials of their own class for the sake of oppressed but alien provincials. Indeed, some provincial governors made it a practice to set aside a portion of their booty to bribe the courts.

VIOLENCE AND REVOLUTIONS: THE LAST CENTURY OF THE REPUBLIC

The deep-seated problems that afflicted Rome produced a century of violence and unrest, between 133 and 30 B.C., that resulted ultimately in the downfall of the Republic and the advent of a new imperial government. The first steps toward revolution were taken by two reform-minded noblemen, the brothers Tiberius and Gaius Gracchus, who advocated a series of popular reform measures and thereby built up a powerful faction among the Roman commoners who were struggling against the entrenched aristocracy of wealth.

Tiberius Gracchus served as tribune in 133 B.C. and Gaius held the same office a decade later. The two Gracchi were deeply concerned with the course of the Republic. Both recognized that the decline in able recruits for the Roman army and the deterioration of morale among the citizenry were caused by the virtual elimination of the small farm from central Italy. Their solution was to create out of the vast public lands owned by the Roman state a multitude of new farms for the dispossessed. This was a courageous and compassionate program, but the virtuous Roman farmer of yesteryear could not be conjured back into existence at this late moment. As it happened, most of the public lands had long before fallen under the *de facto* control of powerful noble families. Long accustomed to farming state lands for their own profit, the nobles reacted frigidly to the proposal that they should now give up portions of these lands so that the state might create small farms for the impoverished. In the political holocaust that followed, both Gracchi were murdered—Tiberius in 133, Gaius in 121. The landed nobility demonstrated that, despite past concessions, it was still in control. But it also betrayed its political and moral bankruptcy. The violence that was now unleashed in Roman political affairs would torment the Republic for a century and finally demolish it.

For a generation the lower classes continued to press for the Gracchan reforms. The landed nobility found itself pitted not only against the masses but sometimes against the equestrian order as well. But the great political fact of the last republican century was the rise of individual adventurers who sought to use successful military careers as springboards to political power.

In 107 B.C. a skillful and ambitious military commander named Marius abolished the long-standing property qualification for military service, opening the army to volunteers from the poorest classes. The property qualification had been diminishing over the previous century in response to a decline in military manpower. Now the process was complete, and the jobless masses thronged into the legions. Military service became, for many, the avenue to economic security, since soldiers of a successful and politically influential general could often expect to receive upon retirement a gift of land from the Senate. The army began to acquire a more professional outlook than before, and soldiers came to identify themselves with their commanders rather than with the state. The opportunities for a ruthless general with a loyal army at his back were limitless.

The subordination of the Roman Republic to the power of generals deepened during the decade of the eighties amidst a struggle between the two foremost commanders of the age, Marius and Sulla. As the architect of open recruitment, Marius drew much of his support from the lesser classes, whereas Sulla tended to ally with the wealthier and more established. But both were motivated strongly by personal ambition.

In 88 B.C., Marius and Sulla were competing for the command of a major military campaign. The Senate awarded the command to Sulla, but Marius, using terrorist tactics, forced a reversal of this decision and gained the command for himself. Sulla, part of his army already assembled, marched on Rome, compelled the Senate to restore his command, and then departed for four years' campaigning in the east. With Sulla busy elsewhere, Marius and his followers resumed control of Rome and slaughtered their political rivals with Assyrian thoroughness. At length, in 83 B.C., Sulla returned from the east and wrested control of the city from Marius' faction—Marius himself having died in the meantime.

In 82 B.C., Sulla took the unprecedented step of making

himself dictator of the Roman Republic. In times of grave crisis the Republic had traditionally concentrated all power in the hands of a dictator, permitting him to exercise virtually unlimited jurisdiction, but for six months only. Sulla compelled the Senate to vote him the dictatorship for an indefinite period, and he used his new power to settle old scores. He tortured and killed many of his enemies and dispossessed others, enriching himself from their confiscated fortunes. But Sulla had no intention of holding power indefinitely. A conservative at heart, he employed his dictatorial prerogatives to establish a series of laws that confirmed and strengthened the power of the Senate, then retired in 79 B.C. to live in luxury on his country estate in Campania, leaving the Republic to stagger on.

In the decade of the sixties, the great senatorial orator Cicero strove desperately to unite senators and equestrians against the growing threat of the generals and the riotous urban masses. Cicero's consummate mastery of Latin style, both in his orations and in his writings, earned him a lofty position in the field of Roman literature, but his political talents proved inadequate to the task of saving the Republic. His dream of reconciling the interests of senators and equestrians was shattered by the selfishness of each, and his efforts to perpetuate the traditional supremacy of the Senate were doomed by the Senate's own incapacity, by the smoldering unrest of the city mobs, and by the power hunger of the military commanders. It was Cicero's misfortune to be a conservative in an epoch of revolutionary turbulence—a statesman in an age of generals.

The Republic was now approaching its final days in an atmosphere of chaos and naked force. The dominant political figures of Cicero's generation were military commanders such as Pompey and Julius Caesar who bid against one another for the backing of the lower classes, seeking to convert mob support into political supremacy. Characteristically, the three great political figures of their age, Pompey, Cicero, and Caesar, all met violent deaths. The failure of republican government was now manifest, and the entire imperial structure seemed on the verge of collapse.

As it turned out, Rome was to emerge from its crisis transformed and strengthened, and its empire was to endure for another five-hundred years. The salvation of the Roman state out of the wreckage of the old order constitutes one of antiquity's most stunning achievements. To this transformation we now turn.

Chapter
12
The Principate

CHRONOLOGY OF THE ROMAN EMPIRE

48 B.C.	Julius Caesar assumes power in Rome
44 B.C.	Julius Caesar assassinated
31 B.C.	Battle of Actium: Octavian (Augustus) takes power
A.D. 14	Death of Augustus
(All further dates A.D.)	
96–180	The age of the great second-century emperors
180–192	Reign of Commodus
193–211	Reign of Septimius Severus
235–284	Height of the anarchy; "barracks emperors"
185–254	Origen
205–270	Plotinus
284–305	Reign of Diocletian
306–337	Reign of Constantine
325	Council of Nicaea
330	Founding of Constantinople

JULIUS CAESAR AND AUGUSTUS

The new order, which saved Rome from the agonies of the late Republic and brought a long era of peace and stability to the Mediterranean world, was chiefly the handiwork of two men: Julius Caesar and his grandnephew, Augustus. Julius Caesar was a man of many talents—a superb general, a brilliant, realistic politician, and a distinguished author whose lucid and forthright *Commentaries on the Gallic Wars* was a significant contribution to the great literary surge of the late Republic. Above all, Caesar was a person of acute practical intelligence who could probe to the core of any problem, work out a logical solution, and then carry his plan to realization.

Caesar managed to ride the whirlwind of violence and ambition that was shattering Roman society during the mid-first century B.C. His political intuition and unswerving faith in himself and his stars catapulted him to increasingly important political and military offices during the turbulent sixties. Opposed and distrusted by the conservative Senate, he allied himself with Pompey, a disgruntled general, and Crassus, an ambitious millionaire. These three formed an extralegal coalition of political bosses, known to later historians as the "First Triumvirate," which succeeded in dominating the Roman state.

Leaving Italy to his two colleagues, Caesar spent most of the following decade (58–50 B.C.) in Gaul leading his army on a spectacular series of campaigns that resulted in the conquest of what is now France and Belgium and established his reputation as one of history's consummate military scientists. Caesar's conquest of Gaul pushed the influence of Rome far northward from the Mediterranean into the heartland of western Europe. The historical consequences of his victories are immense, for in the centuries that followed, Gaul was thoroughly Romanized. The Roman influence survived the later barbarian invasions to give medieval and modern France a romance tongue and to provide western Europe with an enduring Greco-Roman cultural heritage.

While Caesar was winning his triumphs in Gaul, his interests in Italy were suffering. His advocacy of land redistribution and of other policies dear to the hearts of the lower classes earned him the hostility of the Senate. And his spectacular military success threatened to thwart Pompey's own ambition to be first among Romans. Out of their common fear of Caesar, Pompey and the Senate now joined forces, and in 49 B.C. Caesar was declared a public enemy. His career at stake, Caesar defied the Roman constitution by leading his own loyal army into Italy. In a series of dazzling campaigns during 49 and 48 B.C., he defeated Pompey and the hostile senators. Pompey fled to Egypt and was murdered there, leaving the Senate with no choice but to come to terms with the man who now towered unchallenged over Rome.

Caesar was a magnanimous victor. He restored his senatorial opponents to their former positions and ordered the execution of Pompey's murderer. He could afford to be generous for he was now the unquestioned master of the state. Caesar assumed the office of dictator and held it not for the traditional six months, or, like Sulla, with the intention of early retirement, but year after year. Ultimately he forced the Senate to grant him the dictatorship for life. He also assumed the key republican office of consul and retained the title of *pontifex maximus* (supreme pontiff or chief priest of the civic religion) which he had held for some years. In 44 B.C. he received the unprecedented honor of having a temple dedicated to his "genius" (his family spirit), and the month of July was named in his honor. The political institutions of the Republic survived but they were now under his thumb. He controlled the appointment of civic officials, manipulated the assemblies, and overawed the Senate. The whole Roman electorate had become his clients.

Caesar used his power to reform the Republic along logical, practical lines. The magnitude of his reforms defies description. He introduced a radically new calendar that, with minor adjustments, is in almost universal use today. He organized numerous distant colonies that drained off a considerable number of Rome's unemployed and halved the bread dole. He did much to reform and rationalize Italian and provincial government and to purge the republican administration of its abuses. In short, he was the model of what would much later be called an "enlightened despot." Some historians have supposed that Caesar was aiming at a monarchy along Hellenistic lines, but it is more accurate to view him as a supremely talented Roman applying his intellect to the solution of Roman problems.

Caesar's success attests to the creative power of the human mind; his ultimate failure, however, suggests that in human affairs reason is not always enough—that the ingrained historical traditions of a people will resist the surgery of even the most skillful rationalist reformer. Caesar's reforms were immensely beneficial to the people of the Empire, but he went too far too fast. His disregard for republican institutions was too cavalier, and his assumption of the dictatorship for life alarmed powerful elements in the Senate. On the Ides of March (March 15), 44 B.C., he was stabbed to death in the Senate by a group of senatorial conspirators led by Brutus and Cassius. As they rushed from the Senate the assassins shouted, "Tyranny is dead!" They were wrong: it was the Republic that was dead, and Rome now had only the choice between one-man rule and anarchy. By killing Caesar, they had given up the former for the latter.

Caesar's assassination resulted in fourteen more years of civil strife during which the traditionalist party of Brutus and Cassius struggled against would-be heirs to Caesar's power while the heirs struggled among themselves. In the complex maneuvers of this civil war some of the most famous figures in ancient history played out their roles. Mark Antony, Caesar's trusted lieutenant, defeated Brutus and Cassius in battle, and both committed suicide. The golden tongued Cicero, Rome's supreme literary craftsman, was murdered for his hostility to Antony. And when the fortunes of war turned against them, Antony and his celebrated wife, Queen Cleopatra of Egypt, took their own lives.

The ultimate victor in these struggles was a young man who had been virtually unknown at the time of Caesar's death. Octavian, the latter Augustus, Caesar's grandnephew and adopted son, had woven his way through the era of strife with matchless skill and a good measure of luck. A young man of eighteen when Caesar died, Octavian proved to the world that he was in truth Caesar's heir. For although inferior to Caesar in generalship and perhaps also in sheer intellectual strength, Octavian was Caesar's superior as a political realist. During his long, illustrious reign Octavian completed the transformation of the Roman state from Republic to Empire. But his reforms were more traditionalist in appearance than Caesar's, and he succeeded—where Caesar had failed—in winning the Senate's respect. He reformed the Romans and made them accept it.

THE AUGUSTAN AGE

In 31 B.C. Octavian's forces crushed those of Antony and Cleopatra at Actium. A year later Octavian entered Alexandria as master of the Mediterranean world. He was then the same age as Alexander at the time of his death, and it might be supposed that the two world-conquerors, both young, brilliant, and handsome, had much in common. But Octavian refused to visit Alexander's tomb in Alexandria, observing, so it was said, that true greatness lies not in conquest but in reconstruction. It is appropriate, therefore, that Octavian's historical reputation lies not in his military victories but in his accomplishments as peacemaker and architect of the Roman Empire.

The reformation of Rome, completed by Octavian, gave the Mediterranean world two centuries of almost uninterrupted peace during which classical culture developed and spread to the outermost reaches of the Empire. In the turbulent centuries that followed, people looked back longingly at the almost legendary epoch of the "Roman Peace." Octavian accomplished the seemingly impossible task of reconciling the need for one-man rule with the republican traditions of Old Rome. He preserved the Senate; indeed, increased its prestige. He retained the elected republican magistracies. He made no attempt to revive the office of dictator, for he preferred to manipulate the government in more subtle ways. He controlled the army and, like Caesar, he concentrated various key republican offices in his own person. Eventually he went beyond Caesar himself in being granted the power of a tribune (including the right to initiate legislation and the unlimited right of veto, which tribunes had originally exercised in behalf of the plebeian order). With its great flexibility, the tribunician power was ideal for Octavian's needs and became a potent instrument of imperial control. Future emperors dated their reigns from their receipt of it.

In 27 B.C. Octavian was given the novel name of Augustus, a term that carried with it no specific power but had a connotation of reverence—almost holiness. And like Caesar he arranged to have a month (August) named in his honor. The necessity that his month should have as many days as Caesar's July resulted in a permanent asymmetry in our calendar at the expense of luckless February.

Much as Augustus may have enjoyed these various distinctions, he took pains to maintain a relatively modest public image. He commonly used the simple title of *princeps* ("first citizen"), which conveyed the suggestion that he was the leading Roman—nothing more. He lived fairly modestly, associated freely with his fellow citizens, revered the dignity of the Senate, and dressed and ate simply. It has been said that the Principate (the government of the *princeps)* was the mirror opposite of the government of modern England: the former a monarchy masquerading as a republic, the latter a republic masquerading as a monarchy. But if the Principate was at heart a monarchy, it was by no means an arbitrary one. Augustus ruled with a keen sensitivity toward popular and senatorial opinion and a respect for tradition. Ancient Rome, like modern England, had no paper constitution, but it had a venerable body of political customs—an unwritten constitution—that Augustus treated with cautious deference.

Still, Augustus was Rome's true master. The nature of the Empire was such that the liberty of the old Republic simply

Augustus of Primaporta, C. 20 B.C. This marble statue of the young
Augustus is a recognizable yet idealized likeness.

could not be preserved. The Roman electorate was incapable of governing the Empire, and a democratic Empire with universal suffrage was inconceivable. Roman liberty was the single great casualty of the Principate, but its loss was rendered almost painless by the political deftness of the first *princeps*. In its place, Augustus provided peace, security, and justice. The administration of the provinces was now more closely regulated, and the corruption and exploitation of the late Republic were reduced. In Rome itself an efficient imperial bureaucracy developed that was responsible to the *princeps* alone. Although class distinction remained strong, it was now possible for an able person from one of the lesser orders to rise in the government service. And Augustus sought out and supported gifted writers and artists as a matter of policy.

The stable new regime, the promise of enduring peace, the policy of "careers open to talents," and the leadership of Augustus himself combined to evoke a surge of optimism, patriotism, and creative originality. In the field of arts and letters the "Augustan Age" is the climax of Roman creative genius, surpassing even the literary brilliance of the late Republic of which Cicero stands as the supreme example. Under Augustus, Roman artists and poets achieved a powerful synthesis of Greek and Roman elements. Roman architecture was obviously modeled on the Greek, yet it expressed a distinctively Roman spirit. Roman temples often rose higher than those of classical Greece and conveyed a feeling that was less serene—more imposing and dynamic. Augustan poetry—the urbane and faultless lyrics of Horace, the worldly, erotic verses of Ovid, the majestic cadences of Virgil—employed Greek models and ideas, but in original and characteristically Roman ways.

Rome's supreme poem, Virgil's *Aeneid*, was cast in the epic form of Homer and dealt, as Homer's *Odyssey* did, with the voyage of an important figure in the Trojan War. But Aeneas, Virgil's hero, was also the legendary founder of Rome, and the poem is shot through with patriotic prophecies regarding the destiny of the state which Aeneas was to found. Indeed, some readers have seen in Aeneas a symbol of Augustus himself. The *Aeneid* conveys the feeling of hope—that the Roman people,

The Pantheon, Rome, A.D. 118 to 125 (*Alinari—Art Reference Bureau*).

founded by Aeneas and now led by the great peacemaker Augustus, had at last fulfilled their mission to bring enduring concord and justice to the tormented world:

Let it be your charge, O Roman,
  To rule the nations in your empire;
This shall be your art:
  To ordain the law of peace,
  To be merciful to the conquered,
  *To beat the haughty down.**

IMPERIAL LEADERSHIP AFTER AUGUSTUS

Augustus died at the age of 76 in A.D. 14. During the decades following his death the Principate grew steadily more centralized and more efficient. The imperial bureaucracy slowly expanded, taxes were relatively light and intelligently assessed, and the law became increasingly humane. It is a tribute to Augustus' wisdom that the system which he created was sturdy enough to endure and flourish despite the relative incapacity of many of his imperial successors.

The abilities of the first-century emperors ranged from uninspired competence to (putting it charitably) mental illness. We encounter the childish cruelty of Emperor Nero, and the bizarre antics of Caligula, who wallowed in the pleasure of watching his prisoners tortured to death. Caligula is reported to have allowed his favorite horse to dine at the imperial table during formal state dinners, consuming the finest food and wines from jeweled dishes and goblets. At Caligula's death he was on the point of raising the beast to the office of consul. Caligula and Nero were autocrats of the worst sort, and both were removed violently from power. On the whole, however, the emperors of the early Principate retained the traditional attitudes exemplified by Augustus himself, even if they failed to match him in political wisdom.

The second century A.D. witnessed a dramatic improvement

---

*Aeneid, Book 6; adapted from the prose translation of J.W. Mackail.

in the quality of imperial leadership. Rome's rulers between A.D. 96 and 180 have been called the "five good emperors." One nineteenth-century historian described them in these enthusiastic words: "For eighty-four years a series of sovereigns, the best, the wisest and the most statesmanlike that the world has ever seen—Nerva, Trajan, Hadrian, Antoninus, Marcus Aurelius—sat upon the throne of the world."* And although more recent historians would look askance at such sweeping praise, there can be no question but that the "five good emperors" were sovereigns of uncommon ability.

The high level of imperial leadership that characterized this era can be attributed largely to the temporary solving of one of the knottiest dilemmas in the whole imperial system—the problem of succession. In theory the Senate chose the *princeps,* but in fact the succession usually fell to a close relative of the previous emperor and was often arranged by the emperor in advance. Too often this hereditary principle allowed the Empire to fall into the hands of an unworthy ruler; not infrequently a disputed succession was settled by violence and even civil war. But none of the second-century emperors—Trajan, Hadrian, Antoninus Pius, or Marcus Aurelius—came to power by normal hereditary succession. In each case, the previous emperor *adopted* as his son and successor a younger man of outstanding ability.

The policy of adoption worked well for a time, but it did not represent a deliberate rejection of the hereditary succession principle. It was simply a consequence of the fact that none of the "five good emperors" had a son except Marcus Aurelius—the last of them. Marcus followed the hereditary principle—which had never consciously been abandoned—and chose his own son, the incompetent Commodus, as his heir. With the disastrous reign of Commodus (A.D. 180–192) the great age of imperial rule came to an end. It was followed by a century of military despotism, assassinations, economic and administrative breakdown, cultural decay, and civil strife that nearly destroyed the Roman state.

---

*Thomas Hodgkin, *The Dynasty of Theodosius* (Oxford, 1889), p. 18.

THE EMPIRE UNDER THE PRINCIPATE

Before plunging into the troubled third century, let us look briefly at the condition of the Empire at its height. During the two centuries from the rise of Augustus to the death of Marcus Aurelius (31 B.C.–A.D. 180), the Empire expanded gradually to include a vast area encircling the Mediterranean Sea and bulging northward across present-day France and England. It extended about 3000 miles from east to west (about the length of the United States)—from the Tigris-Euphrates Valley to the Atlantic. According to the best scholarly guesses, its inhabitants numbered between fifty and a hundred million, heavily concentrated in the eastern provinces where commerce and civilization had flourished for thousands of years.

Augustus added a considerable amount of territory to the Empire, and several later emperors, notably Trajan, made significant conquests. But most of the emperors were content to guard the frontiers and preserve what had earlier been won. To the east Rome shared a boundary with the Parthian Empire, which gave way during the third century A.D. to a new and aggressive Persian Empire. But elsewhere Rome's expansion from the Mediterranean Basin halted only at the Arabian and Sahara deserts, the Caucasus Mountains, the dense forests of central Europe beyond the Rhine and Danube rivers, the barren highlands of Scotland, and the Atlantic Ocean. In short, the Roman frontiers encompassed virtually all the lands that could be reached by Roman armies and cultivated profitably by Roman landowners.

The burden of defending these frontiers rested on an imperial army of some 300,000 to 500,000 men, organized on principles laid down by Augustus. Infantry legions manned by Roman citizens on long-term enlistments were supplemented by auxiliary forces, both infantry and light cavalry, made up of non-Romans who were granted citizenship at the end of their extended terms of service. The army was concentrated along the frontiers except for the small, privileged praetorian guard that served the emperor in Rome itself.

A high degree of military mobility was ensured by the superb system of roads that linked the city of Rome with its most

Atlantic

Ocean

North

Sea

PICTS

Antonine Wall

Hadrian's
Wall

HIBERNIA

BRITAIN

London

Cologne

12 B.C. to 9 A.D.

GERMANIA

Baltic Sea

Loire R.

GAUL

Lyons

Rhine R.

GERMANS

Danube

Vienna

RAETIA

NORICUM

PANNONIA

PYRENEES

SPAIN

Marseilles

CORSICA

BALEARIC IS.

SARDINIA

APENNINES

I T A L Y

P O

Adriatic Sea

ILLYRICUM

Rome

Naples

Cannae

Tarentum

Actium

GREEKS

M e d i t e r r a n

SICILY

Syracuse

MAURETANIA

NUMIDIA

Carthage

Zama

AFRICA

Scale of Miles

0   200   400   600   800   1000

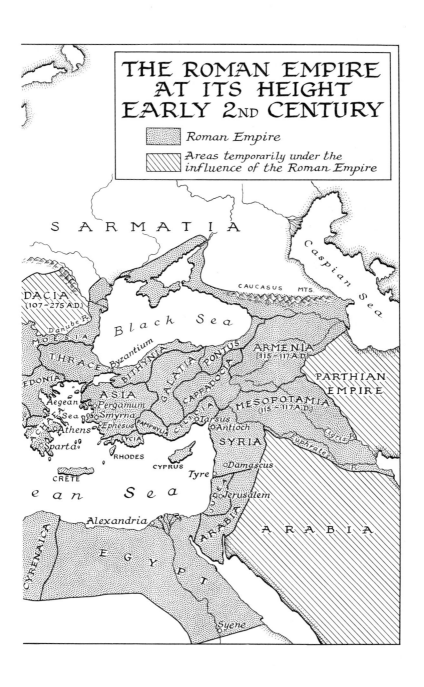

THE ROMAN EMPIRE AT ITS HEIGHT EARLY 2ND CENTURY

Roman Empire

Areas temporarily under the influence of the Roman Empire

S A R M A T I A

Caspian Sea

DACIA
(107-275 A.D.)

CAUCASUS MTS.

Danube R.

Black Sea

MOESIA

THRACE

Byzantium

BITHYNIA

ARMENIA
(115-117 A.D.)

PARTHIAN EMPIRE

PONTUS

GALATIA

CAPPADOCIA

ASIA

MESOPOTAMIA
(115-117 A.D.)

EDONIA

Pergamum

Aegean

Smyrna

CILICIA

Tigris R.

Athens

Ephesus

PAMPHYLIA

Tarsus

Sea

Antioch

SYRIA

Euphrates R.

Sparta

LYCIA

RHODES

CYPRUS

Damascus

CRETE

Tyre

e a n   S e a

JUDEA

Jerusalem

Alexandria

ARABIA

A R A B I A

CYRENAICA

E G Y P T

Syene

remote provinces. Paved with stones fitted closely together, and running in straight lines mile after mile, these roads were nearly as eternal as the city they served. They eased the flow of commerce as well as the movement of troops and remained in use many centuries after the Roman Peace was shattered by anarchy and Germanic invasions.

The Empire's greatest commercial artery was not built of stone; it was the Mediterranean, completely surrounded by imperial territory and referred to affectionately by the Romans as *Mare Nostrum*—"our sea." Roman fleets patrolled the Mediterranean and cleared it of pirates for the first time in antiquity so that peaceful shipping could move safely between the many ports of the Empire.

Under the canopy of the Roman Peace, Roman institutions and classical culture spread far and wide across the Empire. As distant provinces became increasingly Romanized, the meaning of the words Rome and Roman gradually changed. By the time of Augustus these terms were no longer confined to the imperial city and its inhabitants but had come to embrace the greater part of Italy. Later, as the decades of the Roman Peace followed one another, citizenship was extended to more and more provincials until finally, in A.D. 212, every free inhabitant of the Empire was made a citizen. By then, the emperors themselves often came from the provinces: the second-century emperor Trajan, for example, was a native of Spain. In time the terms Rome and Roman acquired a universal connotation: a Greek monarch in Constantinople, a Frankish monarch at Aachen, a Saxon monarch in Germany, a Hapsburg in Vienna could, in later centuries, all refer to themselves as "Roman emperors."

ECONOMIC AND SOCIAL CONDITIONS

The most conspicuous effect of Romanization was the spread of cities across the entire Empire. The city-state, the characteristic political unit of the Greco-Roman world, now extended to the outermost provinces—to Gaul, Spain, the lands along the Rhine and Danube, even remote Britain. The city still retained much local self-government and normally controlled the rural territories in its vicinity. In other words, the city was the key unit of local administration; the government of the Roman state remained fundamentally urban.

Paradoxically, the cities of the Empire, especially in the West, were of relatively minor importance as commercial and manufacturing centers. Although small-scale urban industry often flourished, particularly in the East, the economy of the Empire remained fundamentally agrarian. Many of the western cities, including Rome itself, consumed far more than they produced. Basically they were administrative and military centers whose mercantile significance was secondary. During the first two centuries of the Empire the economy was prosperous enough to support them, but this would not always be the case. In time the cities would decline, and with them the whole political structure of the Greco-Roman world.

By the first and second centuries A.D., the small family farms of the Roman past had given way across much of the Empire to the great *latifundia*—owned by aristocrats and tilled by slaves or half-free peasants. Although the products of Roman farming varied widely from region to region, the principal crops of the Empire were grain, grapes, and olives—the old "Mediterranean triad" that had dominated agriculture in the Mediterranean Basin for countless generations. Grain (chiefly wheat and barley) and grape vines were cultivated throughout most of the Empire. From these the Romans produced two of the basic staples of their diet: bread and wine. Olive trees were also grown in abundance, though their vulnerability to cold restricted their cultivation to the frost-free lowlands around the Mediterranean Sea. The people of the Mediterranean Basin used olive oil in the place of butter, which was favored by the Germanic tribes to the north but turned rancid in the southern heat. Throughout much of Italy, grain production had given way to the raising of grapes, olives, sheep, and cattle. The fertile wheat-growing provinces of Egypt and North Africa had by now become the primary suppliers of bread for the teeming populace of the city of Rome (perhaps 700,000).

In the early Empire, as in the late Republic, slaves played a crucial role in the economy, especially in agriculture. But as the frontiers jelled and the flow of war captives diminished, the chief source of slaves was cut off. Landowners now began to lease major portions of their estates to sharecroppers called *coloni*, who tended to fall more and more under the control of their landlords and sank into a semiservile status akin to that of medieval serfs.

The condition of the slaves, *coloni,* and urban poor should warn us against viewing the Roman Principate, through the rose-tinted telescopes of nineteenth-century historians, as humanity's happiest age. Roman classical culture was impressive but it was also narrowly limited, shared only by the Empire's upper crust. And although everybody benefited from the Roman Peace, the great majority were impoverished and undernourished.

Such conditions persisted throughout the Principate and beyond, not as economic misfortunes that might be remedied by antipoverty programs but as the means necessary for the functioning of great estates, mines, and wealthy households. The leisured lives of the Empire's elite, and the very survival of the imperial economy, depended on the muscles of slaves and poor laborers, who constituted eighty to ninety percent of the total population.

Even the Roman Peace, so widely and properly admired, was not as complete as one might suppose. Germanic tribes hammered repeatedly at Rome's frontiers and sometimes pierced them, while deep within the Empire towns and countryside suffered a degree of local violence and mayhem far exceeding that of modern Western societies. By today's standards, the provinces of the Roman Principate were drastically underpoliced and undergoverned. One historian has recently estimated the size of the professional administrative class across the entire Empire at less than a thousand.

Roman women, even the wealthiest, were forbidden to hold any political office. By long tradition they were expected to stay home and obey their husbands, but many Roman wives declined to meet these expectations. Indeed, in the Empire's later centuries women acquired considerable independence with respect to marriage, divorce, and the holding of property, and upper-class women were often well educated. The Roman father, however, was the master of his family and exercised the power of life or death over his newborn children. If he liked their looks he let them live; if they seemed scrawny or deformed, or if the father already had enough children (particularly female children), they were cast out to die of exposure. This custom of infanticide was yet another brutal consequence of Rome's marginal economy: the Empire could not afford excess mouths.

The imperial economic system provoked no general rebellion because the lower classes knew no better way of managing an empire. Virtually all ancient civilizations were afflicted by mass enslavement, impoverishment, malnutrition, internal violence, the suppression of women, and the killing of unwanted infants (although the religion of the Hebrews prohibited infanticide). In these respects Roman imperial civilization was no worse than the others, and in the larger cities, where public baths and free bread were available, it was significantly better.

Under the second-century emperors, imperial policy was humane and, to a degree, compassionate. It was influenced by the Stoic emphasis on human brotherhood and social and political responsibility. Unlike Caligula and Nero, who used their power to indulge their sadistic whims, emperors such as Hadrian, Antoninus Pius, and Marcus Aurelius viewed their authority as a trust—a commission to govern in the interests of their people, whether rich or poor. They funded charities, provided food to orphans and paupers, launched building programs, and assisted cities in financial distress. Hadrian won wide popularity by canceling all private debts to the imperial government. But given the nature of the Roman economy, such policies could effect no fundamental improvement. Roman life under the "good emperors" could be pleasant enough if one were male, adult, rich, and naturally immune to various epidemic diseases. But if this was humanity's happiest time, God help us all.

THE SILVER AGE

The cultural epoch from approximately the death of Augustus to the death of Marcus Aurelius is known as the silver age. Less celebrated than the golden Augustan Age, it nevertheless produced literary, intellectual, and artistic accomplishments of the first order. Some observers have seen in silver age writers such as the Stoic Seneca and the essayist Pliny the Younger a decline in creative genius. They have stressed the pretentious, ornate style of second-century literature, the stale conformity of second-century art. And they have attributed these shortcomings to the "homogenization" of imperial society and the dullness of peace and security. Such judgments are necessarily relative, and many sensitive people across the centuries have viewed writers of the silver age with enormous admiration.

However one judges the originality of silver age literature, there can be no question but that it produced major works of synthesis. Plutarch (c. 46–120), in his *Parallel Lives,* provided biographies of famous Romans along with notable figures from his native Greece. One of the most widely read works in antiquity, Plutarch's *Lives* undertook to educate youth in the nature of virtue as exemplified by models from both the Greek and the Roman past.

Suetonius' *Lives of the Caesars* is rather less edifying. A treasure chest of court scandal, it educates its reader as much in the nature of vice as of virtue. More significant is the work of Tacitus (c. 55–120), whose histories trace the course of the early Empire carefully and vividly—though from an old-fashioned republican bias. Tacitus also wrote an important study of the early Germanic peoples (which we will encounter again) and a biography of a Roman governor of Britain named Agricola, who was Tacitus' father-in-law.

Throughout the silver age, classical culture spread outward and downward. Remote provincial cities built temples and baths, theaters and triumphal arches in the Roman style. Libraries and schools were scattered abundantly across the Empire, and the extent of urban literacy is demonstrated by the many irreverent and obscene scribblings and campaign slogans discovered by modern excavators on the buildings of Pompeii, buried and preserved by the eruption of Vesuvius in A.D. 79.

Alexandria, the Hellenistic metropolis, retained its commercial and intellectual importance throughout the age of the Principate, producing some of the most brilliant early Christian theologians as well as several distinguished scientists who developed and synthesized the achievements of earlier Hellenistic science. Greek and Hellenistic astronomical thought, as we have seen, was developed into a sophisticated and comprehensive model of the universe by Ptolemy of Alexandria (d. about A.D. 180). Ptolemy also wrote the most complete geography of antiquity, and Galen (A.D. 131−201), a medical scientist from Hellenistic Pergamum, produced a series of works on biology and medicine that dominated these fields for more than a thousand years. The *Meditations* of Marcus Aurelius, the last of the "five good emperors," is a moving expression of the Stoic philosophy that deepened and humanized much of the best thought of the era. In literature and art, science and philosophy, the silver age produced an effortless blend of Greek and Roman traditions. Its cosmopolitanism is echoed in the varied languages, religions, and homelands of its writers. Alongside Latin-speaking Romans such as Tacitus, Suetonius, and Seneca stand the Epicurean satirist Lucian from Syria, the Greek biographer Plutarch, and the Jewish historian Josephus—a Roman citizen who wrote in Greek. In the works of these and other silver age writers, the rich legacies of Greece, Rome, and the ancient Near East were summarized and fused.

ROMAN LAW

Of all the achievements of this epoch perhaps the most far-reaching—certainly the most distinctively Roman—was the development of imperial law. The rigid code of the Twelve Tables was gradually broadened and humanized by the magistrates of the later Republic and early Empire, by the great Roman lawyers of the second and third centuries A.D., and by the enlightened intervention of the emperors themselves. As the Romans became acquainted with more and more peoples, each with its unique set of laws and customs, they gradually emancipated themselves from the peculiarities of their own law and strove to replace it with a body of fundamental principles drawn from the laws of all people. The *Jus Gentium* or "law of peoples" slowly transformed the Roman code into a legal system suitable to a vast, heterogeneous empire.

The evolution of Roman law into a universal system of

jurisprudence owed something also to the Greek concept of the *Jus Naturale*—the "law of nature"—which has played a prominent role in the history of Western thought. More abstract than the *Jus Gentium,* the "law of nature" or "natural law" is based on the belief that in a divinely ordered world there are certain universal norms of human behavior that all people tend to follow, regardless of their own individual customs and traditions. These norms, based on general principles of political and social justice, served to rationalize and humanize the law of the Empire and to provide it with a sturdy philosophical foundation.

Roman law, a product of the Latin practical political genius influenced by Greek speculative thought, gave substance to the Augustan ideal of justice. Codified at enormous effort by the sixth-century emperor Justinian, it has become a crucial part of the Western heritage—the basis of many legal systems to this day in Europe and her former colonies.

Chapter

13

The Spiritual Metamorphosis

ROMAN RELIGION

Roman religion is immensely complex, for the Romans not only recognized many gods but had numerous separate cults. Like the Greek city-states, Rome had its official civic deities—Jupiter and Juno, Minerva and Mars, and many others, who by the later Republic had become identified with parallel gods of the Greek Olympic religion. The Roman Jupiter was the Greek Zeus, the Roman Minerva was the Greek Athena, and so on. Besides these Roman state deities there were the innumerable local gods of the cities and districts of the Empire. And in Rome itself, as well as throughout the Empire, there were countless unofficial cults that enjoyed the toleration of the Roman state. None of these pagan cults was exclusive; none claimed a monopoly on truth, and a single individual might without compromise participate in several of them.

With the coming of the Principate an important new element was added to the state religion: the cult of the emperor. Both Augustus and his successors (with a few notorious exceptions) were deified by the Senate after their deaths. In those provinces where god-kings were traditional, the *princeps* was viewed as a deity while still alive. It became customary for Romans and provincials alike to participate in formal religious observances to the deified emperors as well as to the major deities of the city of Rome. These observances were at heart more patriotic than religious. They were useful in encouraging the allegiance of diverse peoples and, in accordance with religious attitudes of the day, few objected to the addition of a handful of new deities to the divine multitude that they already worshiped.

To the Jews, and later the Christians, these religio-patriotic observances were another matter, for the jealous God of the Jews permitted the worship of no other. But Rome had long recognized the Jews as a people apart and usually excused them from participation in the official cults. The Christians, on the other hand, suffered greatly from their refusal to worship the emperors and gods of Rome. To the Romans such intransigence savored of both atheism and treason. It is no accident that Christianity, alone of all the religions of the Empire, was the object of serious Roman persecution.

THE MYSTERY CULTS

The imperial centuries witnessed a fundamental shift in Roman religious attitudes. The veneration of the traditional gods of household, clan, and city slowly gave way to the worship of transcendental deities imported from the Near East. The gods of Old Rome, like those of Greek Olympus, had safeguarded the welfare of social and political groups; the new gods offered instead the hope of individual redemption, salvation, and eternal life. As the Roman imperial age progressed, religious allegiances drifted from the boisterous and unlikely gods of the

Greco-Roman Olympic cult—Jupiter, Juno, Apollo, Minerva, and the rest—to the Egyptian Isis, the Persian Mithras, the Phrygian Great Mother, the Syrian sun god, and other exotic deities who offered solace and eternal joy.

This surge of mysticism was a continuation and expansion of a trend we have already observed among the Hellenistic Greeks. The same forces that had encouraged rootlessness and disorientation in the Hellenistic world were now at work throughout the Roman Empire: cosmopolitanism, gradually increasing autocracy, and, among the underprivileged majority, grinding poverty and loss of hope. The shift from civic god to savior god, from this world to the next, constitutes a profound transformation in mood. As the peace of the second century gave way to the anarchy of the third, the high hopes of classical humanism—the dream of a rational universe, an ideal republic, a good life—were seeming more and more like cruel illusions, and the movement toward the mystery cults gained enormous momentum.

NEOPLATONISM

The older pagan cults were by no means dead, but they were altered by the growth of otherworldliness that accompanied the third-century anarchy. This trend toward a transcendental outlook is especially conspicuous in the leading philosophical movement of the century, Neoplatonism. The philosopher Plotinus, one of the most influential minds of the Roman imperial era, popularized the doctrine of a single god—infinite, unknowable, and unapproachable except through a mystical experience. This god was the ultimate source of everything, spiritual and physical. All existence was conceived of as a series of circles radiating outward from him, like concentric ripples in a pond, diminishing in excellence and significance as they grew more distant from their divine source. Human reason, which the Greeks had earlier exalted, now lost its fascination, for at the core of reality was a god that lay beyond reason's scope.

Plotinus and his followers regarded the multitudes of pagan gods and goddesses as crude but useful symbols of the true

Neoplatonic god. Though poorly suited to the deepening mood of otherworldliness, the pagan cults were given new life by the overarching structure of Neoplatonic philosophy. They were themselves brought into line with the trend toward mysticism and monotheism. The distinction between Jupiter and the new eastern deities was steadily blurring.

By the fourth century, Greek rationalism and humanism had been superseded almost entirely by a spirit of otherworldliness and a yearning for eternal life. Neoplatonic philosophy and Near Eastern religion were accompanied by astrology, magic, and similar practices which had never been absent from Greco-Roman society but which now dominated popular thinking as never before.

THE EMERGENCE OF CHRISTIANITY

It was in this supernatural atmosphere that the Christians converted the Roman Empire. Some of their beliefs and practices resembled those of older and competing religions: baptism, eternal salvation, the death and resurrection of a savior-god, the sacramental meal, human brotherhood under a divine father—none of these was new. Yet Christianity was more than a recombination of old beliefs, more than simply another of the mystery religions. It differed from them above all in two fundamental ways: (1) its founder and savior was an actual historical personage: compared with Jesus such mythical idealizations as Isis and Mithras would have seemed faint and unreal; (2) its god was not merely the best of many gods but the One God, the God of the Hebrews, unique in all antiquity in his claims to exclusiveness and omnipotence, and now detached by Christianity from his association with a chosen people to become the God of all peoples.

Jesus had lived and died a Jew. He announced that he had come not to abolish Judaism but to fulfill it. In his earliest biographies, the four Gospels, he is pictured as a warm, magnetic leader who miraculously healed the sick, raised the dead, and stilled the winds. His miracles were seen as credentials of the divine authority with which he claimed to speak. His ministry was chiefly to the poor and outcast, and in Christianity's early decades it was they who accepted the new faith most readily. He preached a doctrine of love, compassion, and humility; like the earlier Hebrew prophets, he scorned empty formalism in religion and favored a simple life of generosity toward both friend and enemy, and devotion to God. He did not object to ritual as such, but only to ritual infected with pride and divorced from love of God and neighbor. In the end he was crucified (a common form of execution at the time) for criticizing the complacency of the established Jewish priesthood and claiming to speak with divine authority. The enthusiasm of his followers seems to have alarmed Roman provincial officials, who may have feared a national Jewish uprising.

According to the Gospels, Jesus' greatest miracle was his resurrection—his return to life on the third day after his death on the cross. He is said to have remained on earth for a short period thereafter, giving solace and instruction to his disciples, and then to have ascended into heaven with the promise that he would return in glory to judge all souls and bring the world to an end. The first generation of Christians expected this second coming to occur quickly, which may be one of the reasons that formal organization was not stressed in the primitive Church.

From the beginning, Christians not only accepted Jesus' ethical teachings but also worshiped him as the Christ, the incarnation of God. In the Gospels, Jesus repeatedly distinguishes between himself—"the Son of Man"—and God—"the Father"—but he also makes the statement, "I and the Father are one." And in one account he instructs his followers to baptise all persons "in the name of the Father and the Son and the Holy Spirit." Hence, Christianity became committed to the difficult and sophisticated notion of a single divinity with three aspects. Christ was the "Son" or "Second Person" in a Holy Trinity that was nevertheless one God. The doctrine of the Trinity produced a great deal of theological controversy over the centuries. But it also gave Christians the unique advantage of a single, infinite, philosophically respectable God who could be worshiped and adored in the person of the charismatic, lovable, tragic Jesus.

THE EARLY CHURCH

The first generation of Christianity witnessed the beginning of a deeply significant process whereby the Judeo-Christian heritage was modified and enriched through contact with Greco-Roman culture. Jesus' own apostles were little influenced by Greek thought, and some of them sought to keep Christianity strictly within the ritualistic framework of Judaism. But St. Paul, an early convert who was both a Jew and a Roman citizen, succeeded in steering the Church toward a more encompassing goal. Christians were not to be bound by the strict Jewish dietary laws or the requirement of circumcision (which would have severely diminished Christianity's attraction to adult, non-Jewish males). The new faith would be open to all people everywhere who would accept Jesus as God and Savior—and open to the bracing winds of Greco-Roman thought.

St. Paul traveled far and wide across the Empire, winning converts and establishing Christian communities in many towns and cities of the Mediterranean Basin. Other Christian missionaries, among them St. Peter and Jesus' other apostles, devoted their lives as St. Paul did to traveling, preaching, and organizing—often at the cost of ridicule and martyrdom. Their work was tremendously effective, for by the end of the apostolic generation Christianity had become a ponderable force among the impoverished townspeople of Italy and the East. Within another century it had spread through most of the Roman Empire. The urban poor found it easy to accept a savior who had worked as a carpenter, had surrounded himself with fishermen, ex-prostitutes, and similar riffraff, had been crucified by the imperial authorities, and had promised salvation to all who followed him—free or slave, man or woman.

From the first, Christians engaged regularly in a sacramental meal of bread and wine that came to be called the Eucharist (the Greek word for thanksgiving) or Holy Communion. It was viewed as an indispensable channel of divine grace through which the Christian was infused with the spirit of Christ. By means of another sacrament, baptism, one was initiated into the fellowship of the Church, had all sins forgiven, and received the grace (moral strength) of the Holy Spirit. A person could be baptised only once, and baptised people alone could consider themselves members of the Christian community. But in the early Church, baptism was often delayed until adulthood and many unbaptised persons were therefore associated with Christian communities without being Christians in the full sense. Because baptism erased all sins, some put it off until they were nearing death.

As Christian historical documents become more common, in the second and third centuries, the organization of the Church begins to emerge more sharply than before. These documents disclose an important distinction between the clergy, who governed the Church and administered the sacraments, and the laity whom they served. The clergy, initiated into the Christian priesthood through the ceremony of ordination, were divided into several ranks: the most important were the bishops, who served as spiritual leaders of Christian urban communities, and the ordinary priests, who conducted religious services and administered the Eucharist under a bishop's jurisdiction.* The most powerful of the bishops were the metropolitans or archbishops of the more important cities, who supervised the bishops of their districts. Atop the hierarchy were the bishops of the three or four greatest cities of the Empire: Rome, Alexandria, Antioch, and later Constantinople. These leaders, known as patriarchs, exercised spiritual authority (often more theoretical than real) across vast areas of the Meditterranean world.

In time the bishop of Rome came to be regarded more and more as the highest of the partriarchs. His preeminence was based on the tradition that St. Peter, foremost among Jesus' twelve apostles, had spent his last years in Rome and suffered martyrdom there. St. Peter was held to have been the first bishop of Rome—the first pope—and later popes regarded themselves as his direct successors. Nevertheless, the establishment of effective papal authority over even the Western part of the Church was to require the efforts of many centuries.

---

*The Latin word for bishop is *episcopus*, from which is derived such English words as episcopal (having to do with a bishop or bishops) and Episcopalian (a member of the Anglican communion in America, belonging to a church governed by bishops).

CHRISTIANITY AND CLASSICAL CULTURE

Medieval and modern Christian theology is a product of both the Jewish and the Greek traditions. The synthesis began not among Christians but among Jews, especially those who had migrated in large numbers to the Greco-Egyptian metropolis of Alexandria. Here Jewish scholars—in particular a religious philosopher of the early first century A.D. named Philo Judaeus—worked toward the reconciliation of Jewish Biblical revelation and Greek philosophy. Drawing from Aristotle, the Stoics, and particularly Plato, they developed a symbolic interpretation of the Old Testament that was to influence both Jewish and Christian thought across the centuries.

Following the lead of Philo Judaeus, Christian theologians strove to demonstrate that their religion was more than merely an appealing myth—that it could hold its own in the highest intellectual circles. Plato and the Bible agreed, so they argued, on the existence of a single God and the importance of living an ethical life. As the expectation of an immediate second coming faded, and Christians began to explore their faith more analytically, they began to differ among themselves on such difficult issues as the nature of Christ (how could he be both God and man?) and the Trinity (how can three be one?). Some opinions were so inconsistent with the majority view that they were condemned as "heresies." As questions were raised and orthodox solutions agreed on, Christian doctrine became increasingly specific and elaborate.

The early heresies sought to simplify the nature of Christ and the Trinity. A group known as Gnostics, echoing Persian dualism, insisted that Christ was not truly human but only a divine phantom—that God could not have degraded himself by assuming a flesh-and-blood body. Others maintained that Christ was not fully divine, not an equal member of the Trinity. This last position was taken up in the fourth century by a group of Christians known as Arians (after their leader, Arius), who spread their view throughout the Empire and beyond.

The orthodox position lay midway between Gnosticism and Arianism: Christ was fully human and fully divine. He was a coequal member of the Holy Trinity who had always existed and always would, but who had assumed human form and flesh at a particular moment in time and had walked the earth, taught, suffered, and died as the man Jesus. In this way, the characteristic Christian synthesis of matter and spirit was strictly preserved, and Christ remained the bridge between the two worlds.

The intellectual defenders of early Christianity are known as apologists. In upholding Christian orthodoxy against pagan attacks from without and heterodox attacks from within, they played a crucial role in formulating and elaborating Christian doctrine, coping with problems that had not occurred to the apostolic generation. It is of the highest significance that many early Christian intellectuals worked within the framework of the Greek philosophical tradition. The greatest of them, the Alexandrian theologian Origen (d. 254), constructed a coherent, all-inclusive Christian philosophical system on Platonic foundations. Origen was one of the foremost thinkers of his age. His religious system did not win over the pagan intellectual world at a blow—indeed, several of his conclusions were rejected by later Christian orthodoxy—but he and other Christian theologians succeeded in making their faith meaningful and intellectually attractive to those whose thinking was cast in the Greco-Roman philosophical mold. The greatest of the Greek philosophers, so these Christian writers said, had been led toward truth by the inspiration of the Christian God.

CHRISTIANITY AND THE EMPIRE

At the very time that Christian theology was being Hellenized, pagan thought itself was shifting increasingly toward otherworldliness. Origen's greatest pagan contemporary was the Neoplatonist Plotinus. The growth of a transcendental outlook throughout the ancient world created an atmosphere highly nourishing to a salvation religion such as Christianity. The Christian viewpoint was becoming increasingly in tune with the times; it appealed to an age hungry for a consoling doctrine of personal redemption. Yet its triumph was by no means assured, for it faced other salvation religions such as Mithraism and the

Isis cult—and traditional Greco-Roman paganism in its new, Neoplatonic guise.

Against these rivals Christianity could offer the immense appeal of the historic Jesus, the growing profundity of its theology, the infinite majesty of its God, and the compassion and universalism of its message preserved and dramatized in its canonical books—the Old and New Testaments. Few social groups were immune to its attraction. The poor, humble, and underprivileged made up the bulk of its early converts, and it was to them that Jesus had directed much of his message. Intellectuals were drawn by its Hellenized theology, alienated townspeople by its mysticism, and bureaucrats by the ever-increasing effectiveness of its administrative hierarchy. For in administration no less than in theology the Church was learning from the Greco-Roman world.

Before the collapse of the Roman Empire in the West, Christianity had absorbed and turned to its own purposes much of Rome's heritage in political organization and law, carrying on the Roman administrative and legal tradition into the medieval and modern world. The Church modeled its canon law on Roman civil law. The secular leadership of the Roman Empire gave way to the spiritual leadership of the Roman Church. The pope assumed the old republican and imperial title of *pontifex maximus*—supreme pontiff—and preserved much of the imperial ceremonial of the later Empire. In this organizational sense, the medieval Church has been described as a ghost of the Roman Empire. Yet it was far more than that, for the Church reached its people as Rome never had, giving the impoverished majority a sense of participation and involvement that the Empire had failed to provide.

From the beginning the Christians of the Empire had been a people apart—convinced that they alone possessed the truth and that the truth would one day triumph. Eager to win new converts, they were uncompromising in their rejection of all other religions. They were willing to learn from the pagan world but unwilling ever to submit to it. They angered their pagan contemporaries by their sense of destiny and by their cohesiveness (which doubtless appeared to outsiders as clannishness). Their refusal to offer sacrifices to the state gods resulted in imperial persecution, but only intermittently. Violent purges such as those under Nero and Marcus Aurelius alternated with long periods of official inaction. The persecutions could be cruel and terrifying, but they were neither sufficiently ruthless nor sufficiently sustained to exterminate the whole Christian community, and the martyrdoms only strengthened the resolve of those who survived. (The pagan emperors might have learned much from the Christian inquisitors of sixteenth-century Spain on the subject of liquidating troublesome religious minorities.)

Most emperors, if they persecuted Christians at all, did so reluctantly. The "good emperor" Trajan instructed a provincial governor neither to hunt Christians down nor to heed anonymous accusations. Such a procedure, Trajan observed, is inconsistent with "the spirit of the age." Christians were to be punished only if they were formally accused, tried, and convicted, and then persisted in their refusal to honor the imperial gods. One can admire the Christian who would face death rather than worship false gods, but one can also sympathize with emperors such as Trajan who hesitated to apply their traditional policy of religious toleration to a people who seemed bent on subverting the Empire.

The persecutions of the first and second centuries, although occasionally severe, tended to be limited to specific local areas. The empire-wide persecutions of the third and early fourth centuries were products of the crisis that Roman civilization was then undergoing. The greatest imperial persecution, and the last, occurred at the opening of the fourth century under the Emperor Diocletian. By then Christianity was too well entrenched to be destroyed, and the failure of Diocletian's persecution made it evident that the Empire had no choice but to accommodate itself to the Church.

A decade after the outbreak of this last persecution, Constantine, the first Christian emperor, undertook a dramatic reversal of religious policy. Thereafter Rome endorsed Christianity rather than fighting it, and by the close of the fourth century the majority of the inhabitants of the Empire had been brought into the Christian fold. Rome and Jerusalem had come to terms at last.

Chapter
14

The Dominate

THE THIRD CENTURY

The turbulent third century—the era of Origen and Plotinus—brought catastrophic changes to the Roman Empire. The age of the "five good emperors" (A.D. 96–180) was followed by a hundred troubled years during which anarchy alternated with military despotism. With increased pressures from external peoples, imperial survival came to depend more than ever on military defense. And the Roman legions, well aware of that fact, made and unmade emperors. Roman armies battled one another repeatedly for control of the imperial office until (to exaggerate only slightly) a man might be a general one day, emperor the next, and dead the third. No less than nineteen emperors reigned during the calamitous half-century between 235 and 285, not to mention innumerable usurpers and pretenders whose plots contributed to the general chaos. In this fifty-year period every emperor save one died violently—either by assassination or in battle. The silver age had given way to what one contemporary historian described as an age "of iron and rust."

A crucial factor in the chaos of the third century was the problem of the imperial succession. And all too often the problem was solved by force alone. As the power of the army increased and military rebellions became commonplace, the imperial succession came more and more to depend on the whim of the troops. Perhaps the most successful emperor of the period, Septimius Severus (193–211), maintained his power by expanding and pampering the army, opening its highest offices to every class, and broadening its recruitment. A military career was now the logical springboard to high civil office, and the bureaucracy began to display an increasingly military cast of mind. The old ideals of Republic and Principate were less and less meaningful to those now in power, many of whom had risen from the dregs of society through successful army careers to positions of high political responsibility. These new administrators were often strong and able, but they were not the sort who could be expected to be sensitive to old Roman political traditions. As emperors like Septimius Severus increased taxes to fatten their treasuries and appease their troops, the civilian population was becoming powerless and impoverished. Septimius' dying words to his sons are characteristic of his reign and his times: "Enrich the soldiers and scorn the world."

Back in the reign of Marcus Aurelius (161–180), the Empire had been struck by a devastating plague that lingered on for a generation, and by an irruption of Germanic war bands who spilled across the Rhine-Danube frontier as far as Italy itself. Marcus Aurelius, the philosopher-emperor, was obliged to spend the greater part of his reign campaigning against the invaders, and it was only at enormous effort that he was able to drive them out of the Empire.

During the third century the Germans attacked with renewed fury, penetrating the frontiers time and again, forcing the cities to erect protective walls, and threatening for a time to destroy the Empire. The Germanic onslaught was accompanied by furious attacks from the east by the recently reconstituted

Persian Empire led by able kings of its new Sassanid dynasty.

But Rome's crucial problems were internal. During the third century, political disintegration was accompanied by social and economic breakdown. The ever-rising fiscal demands of the mushrooming bureaucracy and army placed an intolerable burden on the inhabitants of town and country alike. Peasants fled from their fields to escape the tax collector, and the urban middle classes became shrunken and demoralized. The self-governing town, the bedrock of imperial administration and, indeed, of Greco-Roman civilization itself, was beginning to experience serious financial difficulties, and as one city after another turned to the emperor for financial aid, civic autonomy declined. These problems arose partly from the parasitical nature of many of the Roman cities, partly from rising imperial taxes, and partly from the economic stagnation that was slowly gripping the Empire. Having abandoned its career of conquest, Rome was thrown back on its own resources and forced to become economically self-sufficient. For a while all seemed well, but as administrative and military expenses mounted without a corresponding growth in commerce and industry, the imperial economy began to deteriorate. The army, once a source of foreign plunder, was becoming an economic deadweight.

By the third century, if not before, the Roman economy was shrinking. Plagues, hunger, and a sense of hopelessness resulted in a gradual decline in population. At the very time when imperial expenses and imperial taxes were rising, the tax base was contracting. Prosperity gave way to depression and desperation, and the flight of peasants from their farms was accompanied by the flight of the savagely taxed middle classes from their cities. The Empire was now clogged with beggars and brigands, and those who remained at their jobs were taxed all the more heavily.

It was the western half of the Empire that suffered most. What industry there was had always been centered in the East, and money was gradually flowing eastward to productive centers in Syria and Asia Minor and beyond to pay for luxury goods, some of which came from outside the Empire altogether—from Persia, India, and China. In short, the Empire as a whole, and the western Empire especially, suffered from an unfavorable balance of trade that resulted in a steady reduction in Rome's supply of precious metals.

The increasingly desperate financial circumstances of the third-century Empire forced the emperors to experiment in the devaluation of coinage, blending the precious metals in their coins with baser metals. This policy provided only temporary relief. In the long run it resulted in runaway inflation that further undermined the economy and contributed to the crippling of the commercial class. Between A.D. 256 and 280 the cost of living rose a thousand percent.

The third-century anarchy reached its climax during the 260s. By then the Roman economy was virtually in ruins. Germanic armies had burst through the frontiers. Gaul and Britain in the west and a large district in the east had broken loose from imperial control and were pursuing independent courses. The population was shrinking, and the cities were decaying. Pirates once again infested the Mediterranean, and brigands waylaid travelers on the Roman roads. Total political collapse seemed imminent.

As it turned out, however, the Empire was saved by the tremendous efforts of a series of determined leaders who rose to power in the later third century. The Roman state survived in the west for another two centuries and in the east for more than a millennium. But the agonies of the third century left an indelible mark on the reformed Empire. The new imperial structure that brought order out of chaos was vastly different from the government of the Principate: it was an autocracy undisguised by republican trappings.

THE REFORMS OF DIOCLETIAN

Even at the height of the anarchy there were emperors who strove desperately to defend the Roman state. After A.D. 268 a series of able, rough-hewn emperor-generals from the Danubian provinces managed to turn the tide. They restored the frontiers, smashed the invading Germanic and Persian armies, and recovered the lost provinces in Gaul and the East. At the same time, they strove to arrest the social and economic decay.

These policies were expanded and brought to fruition by Diocletian (284–305) and Constantine (306–337), to whom belong the credit—and responsibility—for reconstituting the Empire along authoritarian lines. No longer merely a *princeps*, the emperor was now *dominus et deus*—lord and god—and it is therefore appropriate that the new regime that replaced the Principate should be called the "Dominate."

In the days of Augustus it had been necessary, so as not to offend republican sensibilities, to disguise the power of the emperor. In Diocletian's day the imperial title had for so long been dishonored and abused that it was necessary to exalt it. Borrowing from Greek and Persian court ceremonial, Diocletian and his successors employed all the known arts of costume, makeup, and drama to make themselves appear majestic. Everyone had to fall prostrate in the emperor's presence, and Constantine added the touch of wearing a diadem on his head.

Diocletian's most immediate task was to bring to a close the era of short-lived "barracks emperors" and military usurpers. In order to stabilize the succession and share the ever-growing burden of governing the Empire, he decreed that there would thenceforth be two emperors—one in the East, the other in the West—who would work together harmoniously for the welfare and defense of the state. Each of the two would be titled *Augustus*, and each would adopt a younger colleague—with the title *Caesar*—to share his rule and ultimately to succeed him. The Empire was now reorganized into four administrative regions, each supervised by an Augustus or a Caesar. Well aware of the increasing importance of the eastern over the western half of the Empire, Diocletian made his capital in the East and did not set foot in Rome until the close of his reign. A usurper would now, presumably, be faced with the task of overcoming four widely scattered imperial personages instead of one.

The chances of military usurpation were further reduced by Diocletian's rigorous separation of civil and military authority. He enlarged the army, chiefly by incorporating Germanic forces who now assumed much of the burden of guarding the frontiers. But by restricting the jurisdiction of generals over civilian districts, he reduced their power and enhanced his own.

Imperial control was the keynote of this new regime. The

Senate was now merely ornamental, and the emperor ruled through his obedient and ever-expanding bureaucracy—issuing edict after edict to regulate and systematize the state. The shortage of money was circumvented by a new land tax to be collected in kind. The widespread flight from productive labor was reduced by new laws freezing peasants, artisans, and merchants in their jobs. A vast hereditary caste system quickly developed; sons were required by law to take up the careers and tax burdens of their fathers. Peasants were bound to the land, city dwellers to their urban professions. Workers in the mines and quarries were literally branded.

The caste system was more theoretical than real, for these measures were difficult to enforce and a degree of social mobility remained. Nevertheless, the Dominate was a relatively regimented society. Economic collapse was averted, but at the cost of strict social controls. The once-autonomous cities now lay in the grip of the imperial government, and commitment to the Empire was waning among the tax-ridden middle classes, who had formerly been among its staunchest supporters.

But it was Diocletian's mission to save the Empire whatever the cost, and authoritarian measures may well have been the only ones possible under the circumstances. For every problem Diocletian offered a solution—often heavy-handed, but a solution nevertheless. A thoroughgoing currency reform had retarded inflation but had not stopped it altogether, so Diocletian issued an edict fixing the prices of most commodities by law. To the growing challenge of Christianity Diocletian responded, regretfully, by inaugurating a persecution of unprecedented severity. As it turned out, neither the imperial price controls nor the imperial persecution achieved their purposes. But the very fact that they were attempted illustrates the lengths to which the emperor would go in his effort to hold together the Roman state.

The division of imperial authority among the two Augusti and the two adopted Caesars was a bold, imaginative attempt at political reform. Yet it worked effectively only so long as Diocletian himself was in command. Once his hand was removed, a struggle for power brought renewed civil strife. The principle of adoption, which the sonless Diocletian had revived without serious difficulty, was challenged by the sons of his successors. The era of chaos ran from the end of Diocletian's reign in 305 to the victory of Constantine in 312 at the battle of the Milvian Bridge.

THE REIGN OF CONSTANTINE (306–337)

Constantine's triumph in 312 marked the return of political stability and the consummation of Diocletian's economic and political reforms. In an edict of 332, Constantine further tightened Diocletian's policy of freezing occupations and making them hereditary. He increased imperial authority and embellished imperial ceremonial. But in some respects, Constantine moved in radical new directions. In place of the abortive principle of adoption, he founded an imperial dynasty of his own. For a time he was obliged to share authority with an imperial colleague, but in 324, Constantine defeated his co-emperor in battle and thereafter ruled alone. Nevertheless, the joint rule of an eastern and a western emperor became common in the years after Constantine's death, and he himself contributed to the division of the Empire by building the magnificent eastern capital of Constantinople ("Constantine's City") on the site of the ancient Greek colony of Byzantium.

Constantinople was a second Rome. It had its own Senate, its own imposing temples, palaces, and public buildings, and its own hungry proletariat fed by the bread dole and diverted by chariot races in its enormous Hippodrome. A few decades after its foundation it even acquired its own Christian patriarch. Constantine plundered the Greco-Roman world of its artistic treasures to adorn his new city and lavished his vast resources on its construction. Founded in A.D. 330, Constantinople was to remain the capital of the Eastern Empire for well over a thousand years, impregnable behind its great landward and seaward walls, protected on three sides by the sea, perpetually renewing its economy through its control of the rich commerce flowing between the Black Sea and the Mediterranean. The age-long survival of the Eastern Empire owes much to the superb strategic location of its capital. The lands that its emperors ruled are known to historians as the "Byzantine Empire," after old Byzantium.

Even more momentous than the building of Constantinople was Constantine's conversion to Christianity and his reversal of imperial policy toward the Church. Although he put off baptism until his dying moments, Constantine had been committed to Christianity ever since his victory at the Milvian Bridge in 312. From that time onward he issued a continuous series of pro-Christian edicts insuring full toleration, legalizing bequests to the Church (which accumulated prodigiously over the subsequent centuries), and granting a variety of other privileges. Christianity was now an official religion of the Empire. It was not yet *the* official religion, but it would become so before the fourth century ended.

Various explanations have been offered for Constantine's conversion. He has been portrayed as a political schemer bent on harnessing the vitality of the Church to the faltering state. But there seems no reason to doubt that in fact his conversion was sincere, if superficial. By the fourth century the Empire's mood was deeply religious, and it would be misleading to impose on Constantine the mental framework of a modern skeptic.

THE CHRISTIAN EMPIRE

The respite gained by Diocletian's reforms and the subsequent conversion of Constantine made it possible for the Church to develop rapidly under the benevolent protection of the Empire. In the generations following Constantine's conversion, Christianity enjoyed the active support of a line of Christian emperors. Great aisled churches were built at imperial expense. The combats of gladiators, which had traditionally provided savage amusement for the urban masses, gave way under Christian influence to the less bloodthirsty sport of chariot racing. The practice of crucifixion ceased. And infanticide was prohibited by imperial law. It was repugnant to Christians, as it had always been to Jews, and it was losing much of its social utility in an era of declining population. Slavery continued, for the imperial economy could not survive without it. The Church urged its members to free their slaves, but few were willing to comply and suffer the resulting economic ruin.

Santa Sabina, Rome, A.D. 422-432.

Rich and poor alike now flocked to the Christian faith. Although paganism long survived, particularly in the countryside, Christianity had grown by the end of the fourth century to become the dominant religion of the Mediterranean world. No longer persecuted and disreputable, it was now official, conventional, respectable. And of course it lost some of its former spiritual intensity in the process. Bishops and patriarchs now tended to come from wealthy aristocratic families. And as so often occurs in human institutions, victory was accompanied by an intensification of internal disputes.

Fourth-century Christianity was wracked by doctrinal struggles to such a degree that a contemporary historian, Ammianus, could remark, "No wild beasts are such enemies to mankind as are most Christians to each other." In these theological controversies, as in so many other matters affecting the fourth-century Church, the Christian emperors played a commanding role. It was only with imperial support that Arianism, the most powerful of the fourth-century heresies, was at length suppressed within the Empire.

To orthodox Christians, the Arian belief in Christ's subordination to God the Father was a monstrous perversion of the true doctrine of the Trinity—the equality and codivinity of Father, Son, and Holy Spirit. Constantine sought to heal the Arian-Trinitarian dispute by assembling an ecumenical (universal) council of Christian bishops at Nicaea in A.D. 325. He had no strong convictions himself, but the advocates of the Trinitarian position managed to win his support. With imperial backing, a strongly anti-Arian creed was adopted almost unanimously. The three divine Persons of the Trinity were declared equal: Jesus Christ was "of one substance with the Father."

But Constantine was no theologian. In after years he vacillated, sometimes favoring Arians, sometimes condemning them, and the same ambiguity characterized imperial policy throughout the greater part of the fourth century. Indeed, one of Constantine's fourth-century successors, Julian "the Apostate," reverted to paganism. At length, however, the sternly orthodox Emperor Theodosius I (378–395) banned the teachings of the Arians and broke their power, making orthodox Christianity the official religion of the Roman state. Theodosius outlawed paganism as well, and the old gods of Rome, deprived of imperial sanction, gradually passed into memory.

Although Arianism was now prohibited in the Empire, it survived among some of the Germanic tribes along the frontiers. These peoples had been converted by Arian missionaries around the middle of the fourth century, at a time when Arianism was still strong in the Empire, and the persecutions of Theodosius had no effect on the faith of Germanic tribes. Consequently, when in time these tribes poured into the Western Empire and established successor states on its ruins, they found themselves divided from their Roman subjects not only by language and culture but by bitter religious antagonisms as well.

In accepting imperial support against paganism and heresy, the Church sacrificed much of its earlier independence. The Christians of Constantine's day were so overwhelmed by the emperor's conversion that they tended to glorify him excessively. As a Christian, Constantine could no longer claim divinity, but contemporary Christian writers such as the historian Eusebius allowed him a status that was almost godly. To Eusebius and his contemporaries, Constantine was the thir-

teenth apostle, the master of all churches, the divinely chosen
ruler of the Roman people. His commanding position in
ecclesiastical affairs is illustrated by his domination of the
Council of Nicaea, and the ups and downs of Arianism in the
following decades depended largely on the whims of his successors.

In the East, this glorification of the imperial office ripened into
the notion that the emperor was God's agent on earth. Church
and state tended to merge under the sacred authority of the
emperors at Constantinople. Indeed, the Christianization and
sanctification of the imperial office were potent forces in winning for the eastern emperors the allegiance and commitment of
the masses of their Christian subjects. Religious loyalty to the
Christian emperor provided indispensable nourishment to the
East Roman state over the ensuing centuries. Conversely, widespread hostility toward imperial orthodoxy in districts dominated by heretical groups resulted in the alienation and eventual
loss to the Byzantine Empire of several of its wealthiest provinces.

The veneration of Christian emperors was less marked in the
West, for as the fifth century dawned the Western Empire was
visibly failing. Western churchmen were beginning to realize
that Christian civilization was not irrevocably bound to the
fortunes of imperial Rome. Gradually the Western Church
began to assert its independence of state control—with the
result that Church and state in medieval Western Europe were
never fused but remained always in a state of tension.

In the era of the Christian Empire, the culture of Greco-
Roman antiquity was all but transformed. The sense of otherworldliness, which had long been gaining momentum, produced profound changes in literature and art. Rome drifted far
from the classical Greek culture that it inherited—with its
straightforward, superbly proportioned architecture, its deeply
human drama, its bold flights into uncharted regions of rational
thought, and its tensely controlled, naturalistic sculpture. Greek
classicism had undergone important modifications in the Hellenistic Age and again during the Principate. Now, in the late
Empire, the otherworldly mood brought a virtual transmutation
of the classical spirit.

There had always been a spiritual-mystical element in
Greco-Roman culture, coexisting with the traditional classical

concern with the earthly and concrete. Now the mystical element grew far stronger. More and more of the better minds turned to religious thought, spiritual fulfillment, and the quest for individual salvation. Artists were less interested in portraying physical perfection and more interested in portraying the inner person. The new Christian art depicted slender, heavily robed figures with solemn faces and deep eyes—windows into the soul. Techniques of perspective, which the artists of antiquity had developed to a fine degree, mattered less to the artists of the late Empire (as they have mattered less to artists of our own century). Deemphasizing physical realism, they embellished their works with rich, dazzling colors that stimulated in the beholder a sense of heavenly radiance and religious solemnity. Church interiors shone with glistening mosaics portraying saints and rulers, Christ and the Virgin, on backgrounds of blue or gold. Here was an art vastly different from that of Greek antiquity, with different techniques and different goals, yet just

Mosaics on the nave wall of San Apollinare Nuovo, Ravenna, sixth century A.D., showing a procession of virgins holding their crowns of martyrdom (below), Old Testament Prophets (window level), and scenes from the New Testament (top).

as successful as the art of the Athenian golden age, and more fundamentally original than anything the Roman Empire had done before.

THE DOCTORS OF THE LATIN CHURCH

During the later fourth and early fifth centuries, the long-developing synthesis of Judeo-Christian and Greco-Roman culture was brought to completion by three Christian scholars—St. Ambrose, St. Jerome, and St. Augustine—honored in later years as "Doctors of the Latin Church." Working at a time when the Empire was swiftly becoming Christian, yet before the intellectual vigor of classical antiquity had faded, they used their mastery of Greco-Roman thought to interpret the Christian faith. Nearly seven centuries were to pass before Western Europe regained the intellectual level of late antiquity, and the writings of these three Latin Doctors therefore exerted a commanding influence on succeeding generations.

Although Ambrose, Jerome, and Augustine made their chief impact in the realm of thought, all three were immersed in the political and ecclesiastical affairs of their day. St. Ambrose (c. 340–397) was bishop of Milan, a great city of northern Italy that in the later fourth century replaced Rome as the imperial capital in the West. Ambrose was a superb administrator, a powerful orator, and a vigorous opponent of Arianism. Thoroughly grounded in the literary and philosophical traditions of Greco-Roman civilization, he enriched his Christian writings by drawing from Plato, Cicero, Virgil, and other giants of the pagan past. And as one of the first champions of ecclesiastical independence from the authority of the Empire, he stood at the source of the church-state controversy that was to affect the medieval West so deeply in later generations. When Emperor Theodosius I massacred the rebellious inhabitants of Thessalonica, St. Ambrose excommunicated him from the church of Milan until he should beg forgiveness. The emperor's public repentance set a long-remembered precedent for the principle of ecclesiastical supremacy in matters of faith and morals.

St. Jerome (c. 340–420) was the most celebrated Biblical

scholar of his time. He was a restless man with a touch of acid in his personality: he once remarked to an opponent, "You have the will to lie, good sir, but not the skill to lie." Jerome traveled widely throughout the Empire, living in Rome for a time, then fleeing the worldly city to found a monastery in Bethlehem. His monks devoted themselves to the copying of manuscripts, a task that was to be taken up by countless monks in centuries to come and which, in the long run, resulted in the preservation of important works of Greco-Roman antiquity that would otherwise have perished. The modern world owes a great debt to Jerome and his successors for performing this essential labor.

Jerome himself was torn by doubts as to the propriety of a Christian immersing himself in the works of pagan literary figures such as Homer and Virgil, Horace and Cicero. He was terrified by a dream in which Jesus denied him salvation with the words, "You are a Ciceronian, not a Christian." For a time Jerome renounced all pagan writings, but he was much too devoted to the charms of classical literature to resist their attraction for long. In the end he concluded that Greco-Roman letters might properly be used in the service of the Christian faith.

Jerome's supreme achievement lay in the field of scriptural commentary and translation. It was he who produced the definitive translation of the Bible from its original Hebrew and Greek into Latin—the language of the Western Roman Empire and of medieval Western Europe. The result of Jerome's efforts was the Latin Vulgate Bible, which Catholics have used up to the present century. By preparing a trustworthy Latin version of the fundamental Christian text, he made a decisive contribution to Western Civilization.

St. Augustine of Hippo (354–430) was the foremost philosopher of Roman antiquity. As bishop of Hippo, an important city in North Africa, he was deeply involved in the political-religious problems of his age, and his writings were produced in response to vital contemporary issues. In his *Confessions* he describes his own intellectual and moral journey along a twisting path from youthful hedonism to Christian piety. He writes in the hope that others, lost as he once was, might be led by God into the spiritual haven of the Church.

Augustine wrote voluminously against various pagan and

heretical doctrines that threatened Christian orthodoxy in his age. In the course of these disputes, he examined many of the central problems that have occupied theologians ever since: the nature of the Trinity, the existence of evil in a world created by a good and all-powerful God, the authority of the priesthood, the compatibility of free will and predestination. Out of his diverse writings emerges a body of speculative thought that served as the intellectual foundation for medieval philosophy and theology.

Augustine was disturbed, as Jerome had been, by the danger of pagan thought to the Christian soul. But, like Jerome, he concluded that although a good Christian ought not to *enjoy* pagan writings, he might properly *employ* them for Christian ends. Accordingly, Augustine used the philosophy of Plato and the Neoplatonists as a basis for a new and thoroughly Christian philosophical scheme. As St. Thomas Aquinas observed, looking back from the thirteenth century, "Whenever Augustine, who was expert in the philosophy of the Platonists, found in their teaching anything consistent with faith, he adopted it; those things which he found contrary to faith, he amended."

Plato had taught that abstract ideas were more important than tangible things. He believed that we acquire true knowledge not by observing things and events in the world of nature but by reflecting on the fundamental ideas that underlie the physical universe.* Elaborating on Plato, the Neoplatonists viewed God as the center and source of reality and saw the natural world as merely a dim reflection of its divine source—a faint outer ripple in the concentric circles of existence, scarcely worth considering.

Augustine used Christianity to reshape the insights of Plato and Plotinus. Like the Neoplatonists, he believed that the material world was less important than the spiritual world, but it was nevertheless the creation of a good and loving God who remained actively at work in it. God had created the first man and woman with the intention that they and all their descendenta should attain salvation—should live forever in God's loving presence. But rather than creating mere human puppets,

---

*See pp. 113–114.

God gave humanity freedom to choose between good (accepting his love) and evil (rejecting it). As a consequence of Adam and Eve's choosing wrongly, humanity fell from its original state of innocence, became incorrigibly self-centered, and thus severed its relationship with God. But God reknit the relationship by himself assuming human form in the person of Jesus—suffering, dying, and rising again. The original sin of the first man, Adam, was redeemed by the crucifixion of the sinless God-man, Christ, and the possibility of human salvation was thereby restored.

Accordingly, the central goal of the Christian life is to attain the salvation that Christ has made possible. One can achieve this goal only by becoming a loving, unselfish person, and Augustine insisted that we are powerless to overcome our self-centeredness except through divine grace. He saw us as incapable of earning our own way into heaven. This being so, nobody deserves salvation; yet some achieve it because their moral characters are shaped and strengthened by God's grace.

The necessity of divine grace to human salvation is a central theme in the greatest of Augustine's works, the *City of God*. Here he set forth a comprehensive Christian philosophy of history that was radically new and deeply influential. Rejecting the Greco-Roman notion that history repeats itself in endless, meaningless cycles, he viewed it as a purposeful process of human-divine interaction beginning with the creation and continuing through Christ's incarnation to the end of the world. Augustine interpreted history not in economic or political terms but in moral terms. To him, the single determining force in history was human moral character; the single goal, human salvation. God was not interested in the fate of kingdoms or empires, except insofar as they affected the spiritual destiny of individuals. And individual salvation depended not on the victories of imperial legions but on the cleansing of human moral character by divine grace. True history, therefore, had less to do with the struggles between states than with the war between good and evil that rages within each state and within each soul.

Augustine divided humanity into two opposing groups: not Romans and barbarians as the pagan writers would have it, but those who live in God's grace and those who do not. The former are members of the "City of God," the latter belong to the "Earthly City." The two cities are hopelessly intertwined in this life, but their members will be separated at death by eternal salvation or damnation. Human history, therefore, has as its purpose the growth and welfare of the City of God.

The writings of St. Augustine have shaped Western thought in fundamental ways. His theory of the two cities, although often simplified and reinterpreted in later generations, influenced political ideas over the next thousand years. His Christian Platonism dominated medieval philosophy until the mid-twelfth century and remains a significant theme in religious thought to this day. His distinction between the ordained priesthood and the laity has always been basic to Catholic theology. And his emphasis on divine grace was to be a crucial source of inspiration to Protestant leaders of the sixteenth century.

As a consequence of Augustine's work, together with that of his comtemporaries, Ambrose and Jerome, Christian culture was firmly established on classical foundations. At Augustine's death in 430 the Western Empire was tottering, but the Classical-Christian fusion was now essentially complete. The strength of the Greco-Roman tradition that underlies medieval Christianity and Western Civilization owes much to the fact that these three Latin Doctors, and others like them, found it possible to be both Christians and Ciceronians.

Chapter
15

The Waning of the
Western Empire

THE SPLITTING OF EAST AND WEST

Ever since Diocletian's time, the Roman imperial office had been
split from time to time between a western and an eastern
emperor, and by the end of the fourth century the split had
become permanent. Thenceforth, although the Empire continued to be regarded as a single unit, one emperor ruled the
eastern half from Constantinople while another ruled the western half—no longer from Rome but from some more strategically
situated capital, first Milan, then Ravenna.

This political split reflected a cultural and linguistic division of
long standing. The Latin tongue of the early Romans had spread
across the western provinces, but Greek remained the major
language in the East. (The educated elite throughout the Empire

tended to be bilingual.) To an inhabitant of the urbanized, long-civilized East—Greece, Egypt, Asia Minor, Syria, Palestine—much of Western Europe would have had the appearance of occasional towns and islands of cultivation in an otherwise unbroken wilderness.

During the fourth and fifth centuries, the West's balance of trade with the East grew worse than ever. In exchange for eastern silks, spices, jewels, and grain, the West had little to offer except slaves and hunting dogs—and a diminishing supply of gold coins. Thus, with the coming of large-scale Germanic invasions in the fifth century, the Eastern Empire managed to survive while the political superstructure of the western provinces disintegrated.

THE PROBLEM OF ROME'S "DECLINE AND FALL"

The catastrophe of the "decline and fall of the Roman Empire" has fascinated historians across the centuries, for it involves not only the collapse of one of humanity's most impressive and enduring universal states but also the demise of Greco-Roman Civilization itself. Many reasons have been alleged: climatic changes, diseases, bad ecological habits, sexual orgies, slavery, Christianity—even lead poisoning. None of them makes much sense. Classical Civilization began and ended with slavery, and it was rather less common in the late Empire than in the Principate. Christianity had deeper roots in the Eastern Empire than in the Western, yet the Eastern Empire carried on for another thousand years. As for orgies, the more spectacular of them occurred in the pagan era of the Principate; Christian conversion made them unstylish, and the fifth-century invasions came long after the age of orgies had passed. More significant was the failure of the Roman economy to change or expand, and the parasitical character of the western cities. Then too, the fifth-century western emperors tended to be less competent than their eastern colleagues, and more open to the hazardous policy of filling their armies with Germanic troops under Germanic generals.

The riddle of Rome's "decline and fall" will probably never be completely solved, and even the question itself is misleading. For Rome did not literally fall. Instead, it underwent an immense strategic withdrawal from the less productive West to the wealthier, long-civilized provinces of the eastern Mediterranean. Some historians have found it puzzling that the Western Empire endured as long as it did.

The political collapse culminated in the deposition of the last western emperor in A.D. 476, but the true period of crisis was the chaotic third century when the Empire nearly disintegrated. Viewed against the background of the third-century anarchy, the work of reconstruction under Diocletian and Constantine seems a remarkable achievement. The strong imperial government that emerged at that time became the basis of Byzantine political organization for centuries thereafter and, indeed, made possible the millennium-long survival of the East Roman Empire. But in the West the reforms succeeded only temporarily. The death of the body politic was delayed, but the disease remained uncured.

During the generations after Constantine, the economic problems that had plagued the Western Empire back in the third century grew more intense than ever. Industrial production continued to lag. Instead of importing manufactured goods from major urban centers, the various regions of the Empire tended more and more to produce them locally, and therefore less efficiently. As always, the Roman aristocracy held aloof from trade and manufacturing, preferring to draw their wealth from their great plantations, their status from high public office, and their pleasure from the good company of fellow aristocrats. The Henry Fords and Thomas Edisons would never have been invited to their parties.

The Roman economy remained agrarian to the end, and basic farming techniques advanced very little during the imperial centuries. The Roman plow was adequate but rudimentary, and windmills were unknown. There were some water mills, but nowhere near as many as in, say, eleventh-century England; Roman landowners, continuing to rely on their slaves and *coloni,* seemed little interested in labor-saving devices. The horse could not be used as a draught animal on Roman plantations because the Roman harness crossed the horse's windpipe and strangled him under a heavy load. Consequently, Roman agriculture was powered by oxen, slaves, and peasants.

The economic exhaustion of the Western Empire was accompanied by population decline, runaway inflation, and deepening poverty. The army and bureaucracy grew ever larger. The urban middle classes continued to suffer the burden of higher and higher taxes on fewer and fewer taxpayers until, by the fifth century, the western cities were declining sharply in wealth and population. Only the senatorial aristocracy, the small, exclusive class of great landowners, managed to prosper. As early as the third century they were withdrawing from civic affairs, abandoning their town houses, and retiring to their estates in the country. They warded off marauders and imperial tax collectors alike by assembling armies of their own and fortifying their villas. Having deserted the cities, the aristocracy would remain an agrarian class for the next thousand years.

The decline of the city was damaging to the urbanized administrative structure of the Western Empire. More than that, it crippled the civic culture of Greco-Roman antiquity. The civilizations of Athens, Alexandria, and Rome could not survive in the fields. It is in the decay of urban society that we find the crucial connecting link between political collapse and cultural transformation. In a very real sense Greco-Roman culture was dying long before the demise of the Western Empire; the deposition of the last western emperor in 476 was merely a delayed entombment. By then the cities were shrinking. The rational outlook of Greco-Roman classicism was transformed. The army and even the civil government had become Germanized as the desperate emperors, faced with a growing shortage of people and resources, turned more and more to non-Romans to defend their frontiers and keep order in their state. In the end, Germans abounded in the army, entire tribes were hired to defend the frontiers, and Germanic military leaders came to hold positions of high authority in the Western Empire. Survival had come to depend on the success of Germanic defenders against Germanic invaders.

THE INVASIONS

The Germanic peoples had long been a threat to the Empire. They had defeated a Roman army in the first century; they had probed deeply into the Empire in the second century and again in the mid-third. But until the late fourth century, the Romans had always managed eventually to drive the invaders out or absorb them into the Roman political structure. Beginning in the 370s, however, an exhausted Empire was confronted by renewed Germanic pressures of great magnitude. Lured by the relative wealth, the good soil, and the sunny climate of the Mediterranean world, the Germanic tribes tended to regard the Empire not as something to destroy but as something to enjoy. Their age-long yearning for the fair lands across the Roman frontier was suddenly made urgent by the westward thrust of a tribe of Asiatic nomads known as the Huns. These mounted warriors conquered one Germanic tribe after another and turned them into satellites. They subdued the Ostrogoths and made them a subject people. The other Gothic tribe, the Visigoths, sought to preserve their independence by appealing for sanctuary behind the Empire's Danube frontier. The eastern emperor Valens, a fervent Arian, sympathized with the Visigoths because they were themselves converts to Arian Christianity. In 376 he permitted them to cross peacefully into the Empire.

There was trouble almost immediately. Corrupt imperial officials cheated and abused the Visigoths, who retaliated by going on a rampage. At length Emperor Valens himself took the field against them, but the emperor's military incapacity cost him his army and his life at the battle of Adrianople in 378. Adrianople was a military debacle of the first order. Valens' successor, Theodosius I, managed to pacify the Visigoths, but he could not expel them.

When Theodosius died in 395, imperial authority was split between his two youthful sons. Arcadius, barely eighteen, became emperor in the East; Honorius, a child of eleven, assumed authority in the West. As it happened, the two halves were never again rejoined under a single ruler. Not long after

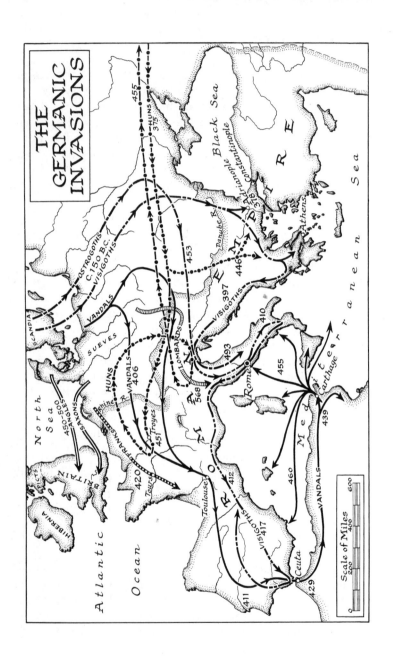

THE GERMANIC INVASIONS

Scale of Miles
0   200   400   600

Theodosius' death, a new Visigothic leader named Alaric led his people on a second pillaging campaign that threatened Italy itself. In 406 the desperate Western Empire recalled most of its troops from the Rhine frontier to block Alaric's advance, with the disastrous result that the Vandals and a number of other tribes crossed the ill-guarded Rhine into Gaul. Shortly thereafter the Roman legions abandoned distant Britain, and the island was gradually overrun by Angles, Saxons, and other Germanic war bands.

In 408 Emperor Honorius engineered the murder of his ablest general, a man of Vandal ancestry named Stilicho. Honorius was by now an adult in his mid-twenties, but the evidence suggests that he was mentally retarded. He apparently suspected, perhaps with reason, that Stilicho's devotion to the imperial cause was less than fervent. But without Stilicho Italy was virtually defenseless. Honorius and his court barricaded themselves behind the impregnable marshes of Ravenna, leaving Rome to the mercies of Alaric. In 410 the Visigoths entered the city unopposed, and Alaric permitted them to plunder it for three days.

The sack of Rome had a devastating impact on imperial morale. "My tongue sticks to the roof of my mouth," wrote St. Jerome on hearing of the catastrophe, "and sobs choke my speech." But in historical perspective, the event was merely a single incident in the disintegration of the Western Empire. The Visigoths soon left Rome to its witless emperor and turned northward into southern Gaul and Spain. There they established a Visigothic kingdom that endured until the Muslim conquests of the eighth century.

Meanwhile other tribes were carving out kingdoms of their own. The Vandals swept through Gaul and Spain and across the Straits of Gibraltar into Africa.* In 430, the year of St. Augustine's death, they captured his episcopal city of Hippo. They established a North African kingdom centering on ancient Carthage and took to the sea as buccaneers, devastating

---

*Historians have had few good things to say about the Vandals, but of course they are no longer here to defend their reputation. We are indebted to them for providing our language with such colorful words as vandal, vandalize, and vandalism.

Mediterranean shipping and sacking coastal cities—including Rome itself. The Vandal conquest of North Africa cost Rome much of its grain supply, while Vandal piracy shattered the peace of the Mediterranean and dealt a crippling blow to the waning commerce of the Western Empire.

Midway through the fifth century the Huns themselves moved against the West, led by Attila, the "Scourge of God." Defeated by a Roman-Visigothic army in Gaul in 451, they returned the following year, hurling themselves toward Rome and leaving a path of devastation behind them. The western emperor left Rome undefended, but the Roman bishop, Pope Leo I, traveled northward from the city to negotiate with the Huns on the chance that they might be persuaded to turn back. Surprisingly, Pope Leo succeeded in his mission. Perhaps because Leo was able to overawe the Huns by his majestic presence, perhaps because their health was jeopardized by the southern heat, they withdrew from Italy—and Attila died shortly afterward. His empire collapsed and the Huns themselves vanished from history. They were not mourned.

In its final years the Western Empire, whose jurisdiction now scarcely extended beyond Italy, fell under the control of hard-bitten military adventurers of Germanic birth. The emperors continued to reign for a time, but their Germanic generals were the powers behind the throne. In 476 the general Odovacar, who saw no point in perpetuating the farce, deposed the last emperor, sent the imperial trappings to Constantinople, and asserted his sovereignty over Italy by diverting a third of the agrarian tax revenues to his Germanic troops. Odovacar claimed to rule as an agent of the Eastern Empire, but in fact he was on his own. A few years later the Ostrogoths, now free of Hunnish control and led by an astute king named Theodoric, advanced into Italy, conquered Odovacar, and established a strong state of their own.

THEODORIC AND CLOVIS

Theodoric ruled Italy from 493 to 526. Though apparently illiterate he respected Roman culture: Arian Ostrogoths and orthodox Romans worked together harmoniously under his governance, repairing aqueducts, erecting new buildings, and bringing a degree of prosperity to the long-troubled peninsula. The improving political and economic climate gave rise to a minor intellectual revival that contributed to the transmission of Greco-Roman culture into the Middle Ages. At a time when the knowledge of Greek was dying out in the West, the philosopher Boethius, a high official in Theodoric's regime, produced a series of Latin translations of Greek philosophical works that served as fundamental texts in western schools for the next five hundred years. Boethius' masterpiece, *The Consolation of Philosophy*, was written at the end of his life, when he had fallen from official favor and was imprisoned. The book's central theme is that earthly misfortunes cannot affect the inner life of a virtuous individual. Although such a notion is consistent with Christianity, Boethius drew his ideas primarily from the thought of Plato and the Stoics. Boethius was himself an orthodox Christian, yet he never mentioned Christianity explicitly in his *Consolation of Philosophy*. Nevertheless, this work remained immensely popular throughout the Middle Ages.

Theodoric's own secretary, Cassiodorus, was another scholar of considerable distinction (though incorrigibly long-winded). A wealthy Roman aristocrat, Cassiodorus spent his later years as abbot of a monastery that he had erected on his own lands in southern Italy. Like Jerome, he set his monks to the task of copying and preserving the literary works of antiquity, both Christian and pagan.

During the years of Theodoric's rule in Ostrogothic Italy, another Germanic king, Clovis (481−511), was carving out a Frankish kingdom in the former Roman province of Gaul. Although far less Romanized than Theodoric, Clovis possessed a keen instinct for political survival. He adopted the straightforward policy of murdering all possible rivals. Gregory of Tours, a sixth-century bishop and historian, quotes him as saying, "Oh woe, for I travel among strangers and have none of my kinfolk to help me!" But Gregory adds, "He did not refer to their deaths out of grief, but craftily, to see if he could bring to light some new relative to kill."

It will perhaps seem odd that Bishop Gregory approved

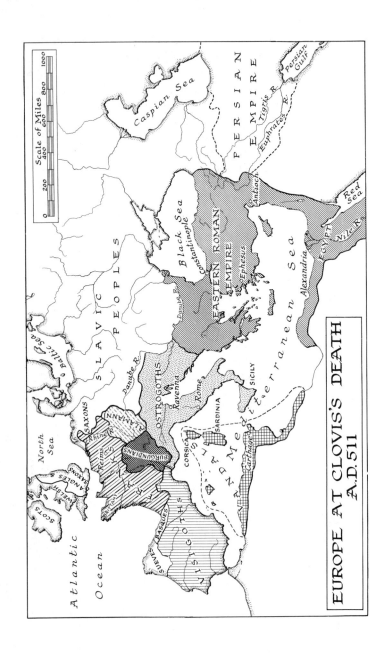

EUROPE AT CLOVIS'S DEATH
A.D. 511

wholeheartedly of Clovis's rule. That savage monarch—who lacked even the family loyalty of a mobster—is pictured in Gregory's history as one who "walked before God with an upright heart and did what was pleasing in his sight." The explanation is that Clovis, having been untouched by Arianism, was converted directly from Germanic paganism to Catholic Christianity. He respected the churches, whereas other Germanic rulers were handing them over to the Arians. Clovis himself regarded Christianity as a kind of magic to help him win battles, but the Church supported him as a hero of Christian orthodoxy.

Another reason for Clovis's good press was that he maintained relatively warm relations with the old landholding aristocracy (to which Bishop Gregory belonged). Because of the depopulated condition of the countryside, there were adequate lands for all—Frank and Gallo-Roman alike. The great landowning families of Roman times were for the most part left in place—to enjoy their fields and their bishoprics, and to serve as high officials in the Frankish regime. From their point of view, Clovis's victory was not so much a conquest as a *coup d' état.*

In succeeding generations Frankish and Gallo-Roman landowners, sharing a common religion, fused through intermarriage into a single aristocratic order. As centuries passed, the royal name "Clovis" was softened to "Louis" and the "Franks" became the "French." And the friendship between the Frankish monarchy and the Church developed into one of the determining elements in European politics.

EUROPE IN A.D. 500

As the sixth century dawned, the Western Empire was only a memory. In its place was a group of Germanic successor states that vaguely prefigured the nations of modern Western Europe. Theodoric headed a relatively tolerant Ostrogothic-Arian regime in Italy. The orthodox Clovis was completing the Frankish conquest of Gaul. The Arian Vandals lorded it over a restive orthodox population in North Africa, seizing the wheat plantations and introducing former aristocrats to the joys of field work.

The Arian Visigoths were being driven out of southern Gaul by the Franks, but their regime continued to dominate Spain for the next two centuries. And the Angles and Saxons were in the process of establishing a group of small, non-Christian kingdoms in Britain that would one day coalesce into "Angle-land" or England.

While Germanic kingdoms were establishing themselves in the West, the Roman papacy was beginning to play an important independent role in European society. We have seen how Pope Leo I (440–461), assumed the task of protecting the city of Rome from the Huns, thereby winning for himself the moral leadership of Italy. Leo and his successors declared that the bishops of Rome—the popes—constituted the highest authority in the Church, and, following the example of St. Ambrose, they insisted on the supremacy of Church over state in spiritual matters. In proclaiming its doctrines of papal supremacy and ecclesiastical independence, the papacy was wisely disengaging itself from the faltering western emperors.

In the fifth century these papal doctrines remained little more than words, but they were to result in an ever-widening gulf between the Eastern and Western Church. More than that, they marked the opening phase of the prolonged medieval struggle between the rival claims of popes and monarchs. The mighty papacy of the High Middle Ages was yet far off, but it was already foreshadowed in the boldly independent stance of Leo I. The Western Empire was crumbling, but eternal Rome still claimed the allegiance of the world.

THE GRECO-ROMAN LEGACY

Notwithstanding the collapse of imperial government, the decline of cities, and the victory of a great Near Eastern religion, Greco-Roman culture never really died in the West. It exerted a profound influence on the fourth-century Doctors of the Latin Church and, through them, on the thought of medieval and early modern Europe. Even the Roman administration survived, through the Middle Ages and beyond, in the organizational structure of the Church. Just as papal Rome echoed imperial

Rome, so too did the ecclesiastical "dioceses" and "provinces," headed by bishops and archbishops, reflect imperial administrative units that had borne identical names. The bishops of the late Empire had become increasingly involved in imperial governance, participating in numerous civic functions and checking on the activities of Roman officials. When the imperial government perished, bishops filled the vacuum by assuming political control of their dioceses, seeing to the maintenance of the food supply and supervising the repair of walls and fortifications. Since most bishops were by then drawn from office-holding families of the old senatorial aristocracy, such duties came easily to them.

The classical past was the source of repeated cultural revivals, great and small, down through the centuries: in the era of Charlemagne, in the High Middle Ages, in the Italian Renaissance, in the northern humanist movement of the sixteenth century, and in the neoclassical movements of more recent times. Roman law endured to shape Western jurisprudence. The examples of democratic Athens and republican Rome inspired the framers of modern constitutions, including our own. (Not by accident was the upper house of the American legislature named "the Senate.") The Latin tongue remained the language of educated Europeans for well over a thousand years, while evolving in the lower levels of society into the Romance languages: Italian, French, Spanish, Portuguese, and Rumanian. And the dream of imperial Rome has obsessed empire builders from Charlemagne to Napoleon.

In these ways and countless more the legacy of classical antiquity has molded our civilization. Across the centuries, the West has been nourished by Greco-Roman culture and haunted by the memory of Rome.

Suggested Readings

GENERAL HISTORIES OF ROME

The two best single-volume textbooks are Max Cary and H.H. Scullard, *A History of Rome down to the Reign of Constantine* (3rd ed., 1975); and A.E.R. Boak and W.G. Sinnigen, *A History of Rome to A.D. 565* (6th ed., 1977). For a lively shorter treatment by a major scholar see Michael Grant, *A History of Rome* (1979).

M. Rostovtzeff, *Rome.* A reprint of volume 2 of Rostovtzeff's *History of the Ancient World* first published in 1927, this scholarly masterpiece stresses social history and overemphasizes class antagonisms.

Other good general studies include R.H. Barrow, *The Romans* (1975); Michael Grant, *The World of Rome* (1960: covering the period 133 B.C.−A.D. 217); and Finley Hooper, *Roman Realities* (1978).

THE REPUBLIC AND EARLY EMPIRE

Thomas W. Africa, *Rome of the Caesars* (1965). The first two centuries of imperial Rome are approached through eleven lively biographical sketches.

Ernest Badian, *Roman Imperialism in the Late Republic* 2nd ed., (1968). Rigorous scholarship; not easy reading.

J.P.V.D. Balstdn has produced a variety of learned and entertaining books: *Life and Leisure in Ancient Rome* (1969); *Rome: The Story of an Empire* (1970: beautifully illustrated); *Roman Women: Their History and Habits* (1962); and *Romans and Aliens* (1980). The last, an account of the Romans' attitudes toward themselves and others, and of non-Roman attitudes toward Romans, reaches the unsurprising conclusion that the Romans thought more highly of themselves than others did.

Emilio Gabba, *Republican Rome: The Army and the Allies* (1976). Translated from Italian, this recent collection of studies by a distinguished scholar of late-republican Rome stresses among other things the importance of the late-republican army as an avenue of advancement for the Italian peasantry.

Michael Grant, *The Etruscans* (1981). A fresh, up-to-date look stressing the marvels of Etruscan art, the immense Etruscan impact on Rome, and the inability of the Etruscan cities to unite against the Romans.

Edward N. Luttwak, *The Grand Strategy of the Roman Empire from the First Century to the Third* (1979). An expert on modern strategic defense presents a fresh, comprehensive analysis of Roman imperial military policy, showing similarities and contrasts to the role of the United States as a world power.

Ramsay MacMullen, *Roman Social Relations, 50 B.C. to A.D. 284* (1974). Paints a more somber picture than the traditional one.

H. Mattingly, *Roman Imperial Civilisation* (1958). A perceptive and significant study.

Claude Nicolet, *The World of the Citizen in Republican Rome* (1980). A masterful portrayal of the civic life of ordinary Romans and their political institutions, translated from the French edition of 1976.

R.M. Ogilvie, *Early Rome and the Etruscans* (1976). A deft summary of recent scholarship and archeology.

Henry T. Rowell, *Rome in the Augustan Age* (1962). Recreates Augustan Rome in social and physical detail.

Chester G. Starr, *The Beginnings of Imperial Rome: Rome in the Mid-Republic* (1980). A very short but challenging reinterpretation arguing that Rome between 338 and 264 B.C. was larger and more active commercially than has been thought.

Ronald Syme, *The Roman Revolution* (1939). A major pioneering work that downplays constitutional factors and stresses the political significance of families and factions in the late Republic.

Malcolm Todd, *Roman Britain* (1981). A learned and readable study that makes full use of both textual and archeological evidence to show the creative fusion of British and Roman culture across the centuries of Roman rule.

Colin Wells, *The Roman Empire* (1981). A brief, up-to-date survey emphasizing the era of the Principate.

THE MYSTERY RELIGIONS AND CHRISTIANITY

Peter Brown, *Augustine of Hippo: A Biography* (1967). A learned study, extraordinarily sensitive to Augustine and his world.

R. Bultmann, *Primitive Christianity in its Contemporary Setting* (1956). This readable and erudite work retains its value after a generation.

Henry Chadwick, *The Early Church* (1967). An illuminating account by a major scholar.

C.N. Cochrane, *Christianity and Classical Culture* (rev. ed., 1944). An interpretive tour de force, sympathetic to the rise of the mystical viewpoint.

Jean Daniélou and Henri Marrou, *The Christian Centuries*, Vol. 1, *The First Six Hundred Years* (1964). This major study combines a Roman Catholic perspective with scholarly objectivity.

J.G. Davies, *The Early Christian Church* (1976). Good scholarship clearly presented.

Michael Grant, *Jesus: An Historian's Review of the Gospels* (1977). A scholarly reconstruction with which not all will agree, stressing that Jesus was perceived as a failure by most of his contemporaries.

J.H.W.G. Liebeschuetz, *Continuity and Change in Roman Religion* (1979). Explores the shifts in religious sentiment from the late Republic to St. Augustine.

R.A. Marcus, *Christianity in the Roman World* (1974). A clear, brief, learned overview from the origins of Christianity to the end of the Western Empire.

THE LATER EMPIRE AND THE GERMANIC INVASIONS

Peter Brown, *The World of Late Antiquity: A.D. 150–750* (1971). A sympathetic study of social and cultural change in Eastern and Western Europe and the Near East, this pioneering work argues persuasively against the notion of a fifth-century break separating ancient from medieval.

Edward Gibbon, *The Decline and Fall of the Roman Empire*, abridged by D.M. Low (1960). A shortened version of Gibbon's eighteenth-century masterpiece.

Walter Goffart, *Barbarians and Romans, A.D. 418–584: The Techniques of Accommodation* (1980). A provocative work that argues strongly against the idea of the Western Empire sinking under a barbarian deluge and stresses the separateness of individual Germanic groups.

Michael Grant, *The Fall of the Roman Empire: A Reappraisal* (1976). Stresses social breakdown as the chief cause.

A.H.M. Jones, *The Later Roman Empire, 284–602* (3 vols., 1964). A major classic stressing social and economic conditions. Jones summarizes his views in *The Decline of the Ancient World* (1966).

Tom B. Jones, *In the Twilight of Antiquity* (1978). Published lectures that explore the period from 326 to 450 through the lives of contemporaries from various levels of society.

Donald Kagan, ed., *The End of the Roman Empire: Decline or Transformation?* (2nd ed., 1978). A short anthology of modern scholarly views, showing that historians remain at odds.

Ferdinand Lot, *The End of the Ancient World and the Beginnings of the Middle Ages* (1961). A reprint of a seminal study stressing the economic factors in Rome's decline.

Ramsay MacMullen, *Constantine* (1969). A good, lively biography.

Lucien Musset, *The Germanic Invasions: The Making of Europe, A.D. 400–600* (1975). Discusses the state of scholarly investigations and controversies; not for beginners.

SOURCES

N. Lewis and M. Rinehold, *Roman Civilization* (2 vols.); and B. Davenport, ed., *The Portable Roman Reader*, are two of several good anthologies now available. There are numerous available editions of the works of Cicero, Livy, Sallust, Josephus, Petronius, Ovid, Catullus, Seneca, Marcus Aurelius, Virgil, Horace, Plutarch, Tacitus, Suetonius, and other important Roman writers, which enable the reader to experience Roman civilization first hand. For early Christianity the New Testament is the ideal source. Modern paperback editions of the four Gospels and the Acts of the Apostles are readily available. St. Augustine's *Confessions* has been published in several paperback editions. For the *City of God*, see Vernon J. Bourke, ed., *St. Augustine's City of God* (an intelligent abridgment), and for a nearly contemporary account of Clovis and the early Franks see Gregory of Tours, *History of the Franks*, tr. Ernest Brehaut.

Photo Credits

Index